This Lenten season and Easter, explore the biblical, historical, and cultural origins of the world's most beloved traditions for this sacred time of year.

Each daily reading—free of religious jargon—is perfect for personal devotions, complete with inspiring words to absorb, quotes to contemplate, and poetry to enjoy.

Short and celebratory, HE IS RISEN is sure to rekindle the significance of Lent and Easter in Christians and draw seekers to take a fresh look at the celebration.

HE IS RISEN

also by Richard Abanes

What Every Parent Needs to Know About Video Games

The Truth Behind the DaVinci Code

also by Richard and Evangeline Abanes

Homeland Insecurity: A Novel

HE IS RISEN

Reflections on Easter and the Forty Days of Lent

Richard Abanes

NEW YORK BOSTON NASHVILLE

FaithWords
Hachette Book Group USA
237 Park Avenue
New York, NY 10017

Visit our Web site at www.faithwords.com.

Printed in Singapore

FIRST EDITION: FEBRUARY 2008
10 9 8 7 6 5 4 3 2

FaithWords is a division of Hachette Book Group USA, Inc. The FaithWords name and logo is a trademark of Hachette Book Group USA, Inc.

Book design by Fearn Cutler de Vicq

Library of Congress Cataloging-in-Publication Data

Abanes, Richard.
He is risen : reflections on Easter and the forty days of Lent / Richard Abanes.—1st ed.
p. cm.
ISBN-13: 978-0-446-69679-1
ISBN-10: 0-446-69679-X
1. Easter—Meditations. 2. Lent—Meditations.
I. Title.
BV55.A23 2008
242'.34—dc22

2007021360

Mom and Dad,
Happy Easter.

Acknowledgments

Thank You
Steve Laube

Contents

CELEBRATING A MIRACLE xvii

WEEK ONE

The Celebration Begins

Sunday **Out of the Frying Pan** 3

Monday **Marked for Redemption** 7

Fat Tuesday **A Time of Sacrifice** 11

Ash Wednesday **Spring Cleaning** 15

Thursday **Pray Without Ceasing** 21

Friday **Making Amends** 27

Saturday **Doing Good** 31

WEEK TWO

At the Cross

Sunday **Tearing Down Walls** 37

Monday **The Perfect Gift** 39

Tuesday **Morning by Morning** 43

Wednesday **For This Purpose He Came** 49

Thursday **You Were a Slave** 55

Friday **An Extension of Credit** 61

Saturday **Reaping the Harvest** 65

WEEK THREE

Reasons to Believe

Sunday **Skeptics among Us** 71

Monday **Did He Fake It?** 77

Tuesday **A Conspiracy Theory** 85

Wednesday **The Jesus Impersonator?** 89

Thursday **More Than a Spirit** 93

Friday **A Skeptic Believes** 97

Saturday **The Evidence Is In** 99

WEEK FOUR

The Meanings of Easter

Sunday **Just the Facts** 107

Monday **When Is Easter?** 113

Tuesday **Spreading the Good News** 117

Wednesday **Double Meanings** 121

Thursday **A World of Difference** 127

Friday **Heavenly Signs** 129

Saturday **All Creatures Great and Small** 133

WEEK FIVE

Signs and Wonders

Sunday **The Flora of Easter** 141

Monday **The Legend of the Dogwood** 145

Tuesday **A Sand Dollar's Tale** 149

Wednesday **The Mythical Phoenix** 155

Thursday **Believing in the Easter Bunny** 159

Friday **The Incredible, Edible Symbol** 165

Saturday **The Colors of Faith** 171

WEEK SIX

A Time for Traditions

Sunday **Hot Cross Buns** 179

Monday **Blessing of the Baskets** 183

Tuesday **Hosanna! Hosanna!** 189

Wednesday **Where Jesus Walked** 195

Thursday **No Greater Love** 197

Friday **What's So Good About Friday?** 201

Saturday **A New Fire** 207

HOLY WEEK
The Human Drama

Palm Sunday **An Altar in Our Homes** 215

Monday **The Passion of the Christ** 223

Tuesday ***Viva Cristo Rey!*** 227

Wednesday **To Bear His Burdens** 229

Maundy Thursday **Fireworks for Jesus** 235

Good Friday **A New Life; A New Look** 239

Holy Saturday **On the Horizon** 243

Easter Sunday **Oh, Happy Day!** 249

REFERENCES 255

PERMISSIONS 263

Celebrating a Miracle

T'was Easter-Sunday. The full-blossomed trees
Filled the air with fragrance and with joy.

Henry Wadsworth Longfellow
1807–1882
American poet

Next to Christmas, my favorite holiday as a young boy was Easter. It was a season of decorating eggs with my family, giving baskets of homemade goodies to friends, and visiting the mall's six-foot-two-inch white bunny who passed out *free* candy. I'll never forget sprinting around a field or yard, my eyes peeled for those elusive stashes of brightly colored hard-boiled treasures, hoping to find the coveted, one-of-a-kind speckled egg.

Then came the Easter feast. I will forever remember the yearly sight of my Gran-Gran's dinner table, lusciously laden from end-to-end with delectable foods, carefully prepared and lovingly presented in piping hot pots and on sizzling plates. We formed a line to go around to each dish, taking more than enough to fill our stomachs. The choices seemed endless: glazed ham, turkey, mashed potatoes and homemade gravy, rice, green beans, yams with cinnamon, and corn on the cob. After all of that came dessert: pies, pies, pies . . . then more pies.

Over the years, little has changed in the way we celebrate Easter in America. Egg hunts, gift baskets, and Sunday feasts are as popular as ever and provide immeasurable joy to children and adults alike. But, there is far more to Easter. For Christians worldwide, the holiday celebrates the faith's foundational event and doctrinal cornerstone:

the resurrection of Jesus of Nazareth three days after his crucifixion. The importance of this miracle cannot be overstated. As Paul the apostle explained, "If Christ has not been raised, your faith is futile" (1 Corinthians 15:17 NIV).

Given the pivotal nature of the resurrection, it is not difficult to see why followers of the Man from Galilee have set aside a day to commemorate his glorious return to life. That singularly wondrous event simultaneously confirmed Christ's authority over death, proved his divinity in the eyes of witnesses, fulfilled Old Testament prophecies concerning the Messiah, and made possible the salvation of all those who, by faith, accept his sacrifice on the cross for their sins.

Easter is a holy day that embodies the very heart and soul of the Christian gospel—the Good News that Christ lives. "For what I received I passed on to you as of first importance: that Christ died for our sins according to the Scriptures, that he was buried, and he was raised on the third day" (1 Corinthians 15:3–4 NIV). We, too, can live, as Jesus himself emphatically declares in John 11:25, "I am the resurrection and the life. He who believes in me will live, even though he dies" (NIV).

If there is anything on the earth worth celebrating, it is surely this promise. Consider the thoughts of distinguished Bible teacher J. Dwight Pentecost, who aptly summarized the meaning of the Easter miracle in his book *Things Which Become Sound Doctrine*:

> Since Jesus Christ is raised from the dead, we who have received Him as Savior have the assurance that sins have been forgiven and that the next step in the program is resurrection into His glory. . . . So there is victory through the resurrection

> of Christ—victory over sin, victory over defeat, victory over despair, victory over fear—because Christ hath been raised and He said, "If I live, ye shall live also." This is the message of certainty and hope that we have. . . . [S]hould death be our experience, we rest in hope, for death has been robbed of its venom because Christ has been raised from the dead.

Christians have adopted a myriad of ways to observe the holy day of Easter and depict Christ's victory over death. Some of them are ancient, while others are far more recent in origin. All of them, however, point to the inescapable message of Christianity—Christ is risen!

This book is a series of readings meant to not only bring the Easter story to life, but also to highlight many of the customs, traditions, and symbols that have come to represent

Jesus' resurrection. My hope is that by looking at what happened on that initial Easter Sunday and at how that event continues to be celebrated, we can find a new level of appreciation for the holiday and what it represents to Christians.

Following the Christian calendar for the season, our short meditations will lead us day by day toward the crucifixion and ultimately to Resurrection Sunday. It is a path that untold numbers of Christians have been walking for 2,000 years. Enjoy the journey!

On a hill far away stood an old rugged cross,
The emblem of suffering and shame;
And I love that old cross, where the dearest
and best,
For a world of lost sinners was slain.

George Bennard
1873–1978
American hymnist

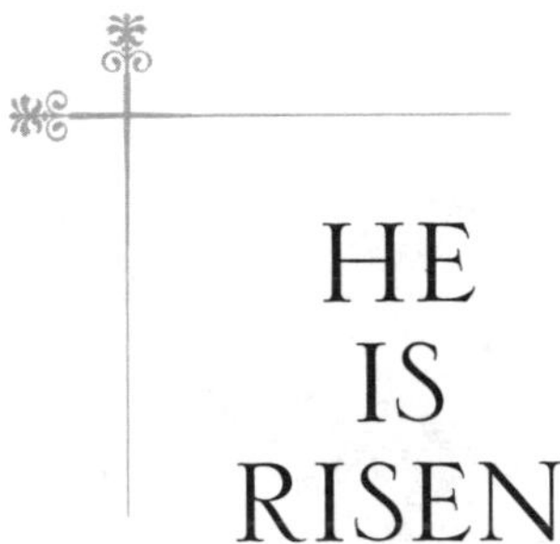

HE IS RISEN

Week One

The Celebration Begins

Out of the Frying Pan

The Tale of Pancake Tuesday

"Now John's disciples and the Pharisees were fasting. Some people came and asked Jesus, 'How is it that John's disciples and the disciples of the Pharisees are fasting, but yours are not?' Jesus answered, 'How can the guests of the bridegroom fast while he is with them?' "

Mark 2:18–19 NIV

To prepare themselves spiritually for Easter, Christians observe Lent—a time of fasting, charity and reflection. This is why, in many parts of the world, the day before Ash Wednesday (when the Lenten fast begins), is devoted to feasting. In England, Australia, and Ireland, for example, the Easter season begins on Pancake Tuesday. This name derives from the old custom of removing the eggs, flour, milk and fats from the kitchen in preparation for the Lenten fast.

To use up these items, in the days before modern preservation methods became available, cooks made pancakes for the day's meals. Pancakes are still made today, shared with families and friends, and are sometimes sold at community functions to raise money to donate to charities during Lent.

Pancake Tuesday is also known as Shrove Tuesday after the tradition of confessing one's sins to someone before Lent starts. To *shrive* in Old English means to absolve (or forgive) the sins of someone else, a practice that, in the Middle Ages, coincided with the ringing of the "Pancake Bell" that called everyone to confession. It also signaled families to begin making their batter for a pancake lunch. In many cities and towns, this custom of ringing the

Shrove Bell continues, much to the delight of twenty-first century celebrants.

Pancake races are also a major part of many pre-Lenten festivities. Participants run a lengthy course from the market square to church, carrying a pancake in a pan and flipping it over at least three times during the race. The most famous race has been held in the small town of Olney, England, since 1445.

It all began, so the story goes, when a townswoman was so busy making pancakes that she lost track of time. After hearing the Shriving Bell, she ran all the way from her house to the church still wearing her apron and holding her frying pan!

In Norway, the Easter season begins with a three-day festival that starts on the Sunday before Ash Wednesday. This period—known as Shrovetide—includes Sunday, Blå-mandag (Blue) Monday, and Fetetirsdag

(Fattening) Tuesday (so named after the "fats" removed from the kitchen. Cooks can use them up in meals before the Lenten fast begins the next day).

Finland likewise views Shrove Tuesday as a major holiday. To celebrate, many schoolchildren are released from class so they can go tobogganing. It is also customary for youngsters there to recite traditional poems that address the people's hopes for a bountiful year of crops.

Marked for Redemption

Origins of Ash Wednesday

All go to the same place; all come from dust, and to dust all return.

Ecclesiastes 3:20 NIV

Ash Wednesday, which originated somewhere in the mid-seventh century, is the first day of Lent. It gets its name from the custom of placing ashes in the shape of a cross on the foreheads of Christians to symbolize their mortality. This act is typically accompanied by a variant of the phrase, "Remember, oh man, that dust you are, and to dust you shall return." The words are based on biblical passages, Genesis 3:19 and Ecclesiastes 3:20. The latter says, "All go to the same place; all come from dust, and to dust all return" (Ecclesiastes 3:20 NIV).

According to the *Dictionary of Biblical Imagery,* ashes were associated with death due to "the ancient military practice of burning enemy cities." Consider Jeremiah's depiction: "The whole valley where dead bodies and ashes are thrown, and all the terraces out to the Kidron Valley on the east as far as the corner of the Horse Gate will be holy to the Lord. The city will never be uprooted or demolished" (Jeremiah 31:40 NIV).

Ashes are also a sign of penitence and/or mourning. This is based on biblical verses where individuals are shown putting dust/ashes on their heads to demonstrate sorrow. In the Old Testament, for example, we see Job expressing grief over his sinful state of mind. "Therefore I despise myself and repent in dust and ashes" (Job 42:6 NIV). This same book of the Bible also depicts the use of ashes (or dust) by individuals mourning a particularly grievous situation: "When they saw him from a distance, they could hardly recognize him; they began to weep aloud, and they tore their robes and sprinkled dust on their heads" (Job 2:12 NIV).

And in the New Testament we have the widespread sins of an entire nation being lamented with ashes: "Woe to you, Korazin! Woe to you, Bethsaida! If the miracles that were performed in you had been performed in Tyre and Sidon, they would have repented long ago in sackcloth and ashes" (Matthew 11:21 NIV).

As for putting a cross of ashes on the forehead, this symbolizes the spiritual seal that God places on candidates at baptism. It represents the new spiritual mark of ownership when a believer is transformed from being a slave to Satan in his kingdom of darkness, to being a slave of righteousness in God's kingdom of light.

This was expressed most clearly by Paul

the apostle. "You have been set free from sin and have become slaves to righteousness" (Romans 6:18 NIV). "And do not grieve the Holy Spirit of God, with whom you were sealed for the day of redemption."

A Time of Sacrifice

The Lenten Fast

The tempter came to him and said, "If you are the Son of God, tell these stones to become bread." Jesus answered, "It is written: 'Man does not live on bread alone, but on every word that comes from the mouth of God.'"

Matthew 4:3–4 NIV

The earliest reference to the forty days of Lent (which comes from the modern German word Lenz or "spring"), is found in the fifth canon of the Council of Nicea. Today most Christian denominations and independent groups observe Lent—Eastern Orthodox, Anglican, Roman Catholic, Lutheran, Methodist, Presbyterian and evangelical, to name but a few. It is a sacred season of devotion to God when believers concentrate on fasting, prayer, acts of penance/penitence, and works of charity. The Lenten period actually totals forty-six days, but because none of the six Sundays that fall during the season count as days of fasting, the actual number of days viewed as "Lent" are the other forty days.

The practice of fasting before Easter appears to have grown out of the early custom of holding baptisms at Pascha (the Greek translation of the Hebrew word Pesah, or passover). This fast served as a time of reflection for the converts to focus their thoughts on the ultimate sacrifice Christ had made for them.

Eventually, Christians adopted a forty-day fast as parallel to the fasting/temptation that Jesus endured in the wilderness. "Then Jesus was led by the Spirit into the desert to be tempted by the devil. He fasted forty days and forty nights, he was hungry" (Matthew 4:1–2 NIV).

When this tradition began, the fast was rather stringent. Only one meal was eaten per day, and even then, "all flesh and 'white meats'" were forbidden, notes Howard Sainsbury, in his entry "Lent," in *The New International Dictionary of the Christian Church.*

These guidelines, however, were gradually relaxed. Now, the Lenten fast can range from eating one meal a day to taking regular meals, but abstaining from a favorite food or beverage (for example, chocolate or soda) throughout the season. In some communities, the "fast" applies neither to food nor to drink, but instead, to a favorite activity or hobby (for example, watching television or listening to music). The time normally spent dining or enjoying a hobby is instead devoted to pursuing a closer walk with the Lord through Bible study, prayer, the reading of some Christian book (for example, *My Utmost for His Highest* by Oswald Chambers) or any other spiritual act.

Despite such modern twists on the ancient fast, its spiritual purposes remain unchanged. A person's self-denial shows a willingness to make a sacrifice to God, just as Christ was willing to sacrifice himself. Moreover, fasting during Lent is intended to draw one's focus away from earthly desires. This way the entire heart, mind, and soul can reflect on God and thereby grow closer to Christ. In other words, the Christian seeks "a change of heart during Lent in their relationship to God," concludes T. J. German, in his article "Lent," from the *Evangelical Dictionary of Theology*.

Spring Cleaning

Praying in the Wilderness

"All this I will give you," he said, "if you will bow down and worship me." Jesus said to him, "Away from me, Satan! For it is written: 'Worship the Lord your God, and serve Him only.'"

Matthew 4:9–10 NIV

Prayer is closely linked to fasting, especially during the Easter season. In the Armenian Church, for example, both prayer and fasting are directly tied together through Matthew 4, which speaks of Jesus enduring his forty days of fasting in the wilderness and the temptations he faced from Satan. "The Meaning of Lent," an article on the Armenian

Church Web site (www.armenianchurch.net) explains:

> During Lent, we go into our own inner wilderness—caused by sins, spiritual laziness, and empty vanity. There we confront the devil. Through prayer, fasting, Bible reading, and self-examination, we gain the strength to work at being more loving, humble, and gentle: the beautiful fruit of the resurrection, which is life Everlasting with Christ our Lord.

Many Christians often use a very short prayer to meditate on, saying it aloud or silently throughout the day. Consider these Lenten prayers published by the Evangelical Lutheran Church in America:

> Jesus, who knew temptation and hunger for our sake: Free us from all covetousness, and wake us from indifference to evil. . . .

Eternal God, whose image we bear: You have created us to live by more than bread alone [Matthew 4:4]. Nourish us through your Word and release us from selfishness born of fear. . . .

Christ, who wept over Jerusalem: Look with compassion upon the cities of our time; that our children might live to adulthood and enjoy a future filled with hope. . . .

God, who searches for the lost: our season brings the lengthening of days and longer light reveals what had been hidden. Cleanse our hearts as we spring-clean our dwellings, that we give away what we no longer need and justice and kindness have ample room . . .

As we approach God in hopes of growing closer to him and deepening our walk with Christ there is no end to what we can pray about during Lent. One Web site that provides resources and information for ministers, elders, and members of the Church of Scotland lists numerous prayers for Christian living in the spirit of the Lenten season. Topics include: increased faith, repentance, obedience, forgiveness, self-sacrifice, holiness, purity, kindness, spiritual maturity, and love toward God and others. Visit "Short Prayers for Lent" (www.kirkweb.org).

The entire message of Lent is one of faith, hope, and love, paying special attention to one's personal relationship with God. "But the greatest of these is love" (1 Corinthians 13:13 NIV). It is a time of "intense spiritual housecleaning" and "letting go of the bondage of sin" say the articles "All About Lent" and "The Season of Lent" (see www.churchyear.net and www.sundayschoollessons.com).

The Reverend George Mastrantonis of the Greek Orthodox Church in America has given perhaps the most poignant definition of Lent in "The Great Lent: A Week by Week Meaning." He calls it "a 'workshop' where the character of the faithful is spiritually uplifted and strengthened; where his life is rededicated to the principles and ideals of the gospel; where the faith culminates in deep conviction of life; where apathy and disinterest turn into vigorous activities of faith and good works."

Pray Without Ceasing
Weekly Prayers for Lent

Is any one of you in trouble? He should pray. Is anyone happy? Let him sing songs of praise. Are any one of you sick? He should call the elders of the church to pray over him and anoint him with oil in the name of the Lord. And the prayer offered in faith will make the sick person well, the Lord will raise him up. If he has sinned, he will be forgiven. Therefore; confess your sins to each other and pray for each other so that you may be healed. The prayer of a righteous man is powerful and effective.

James 5:13–16 NIV

In this time of fasting, reflection, introspection, and meditation on God, the goal is to have a closer walk with the Lord by the time Resurrection Sunday arrives; then to experience another year in Christ with greater joy, deeper commitment, and a better understanding of our purpose in life as servants of Jesus of Nazareth.

Prayer, as mentioned in the last chapter, is the most obvious way to accomplish this. But elaborate expressions are not necessary. The best prayers are often the shortest—whispered while stuck in traffic, riding an elevator, or getting ready for work. The following prayers, for instance, are suitable anytime throughout the days of Lent and can be recited anywhere. Each one should be a "prayer of the moment" so to speak.

Week One: Dear Jesus, as Lent begins, enable me, by the power of your Holy Spirit, once again to seek you above all other things. Help me to love you with all my heart, soul, mind, and strength. Forgive me for those times since last Easter when I have forgotten about you, or lived in a way that did not honor you. I want to grow closer than I have ever been in the past.

Week Two: Precious Lord, throughout this week I pray that you would reveal to me those areas of my life where I have not been faithful to you. I know that my heart is tainted by sin and that only you can reveal its darkest places to me. Shine your light where it needs to shine so I can see my weaknesses and failures, confess them, and move on toward a deeper relationship with you.

Week Three: God, help me to make right any wrongs that I have done during the past year. If I need to seek forgiveness from anyone, give me the courage to ask for it. If I have feelings of bitterness or anger in my heart toward anyone, give me the strength

I need to face them, release those feelings by telling them how I feel and forgive them. And if I have harmed anyone, show me how I can make it up to them. Remove everything in my life that is keeping me from having a pure heart before you.

Week Four: Heavenly Father, show me how I can be of service to you. I don't want to live just for myself anymore, but I want to have a purpose in life that rests in your hands and is under your control. Show me how I can stop living just for myself, and start living for others as a representative of Jesus. I want your Son's love to flow through me so that the kingdom of God will be present wherever I may be.

Week Five: Lord, lay on my heart anyone for whom you may wish me to pray. Whether it is a family member, a friend, a co-worker, or even a stranger I might happen to pass on the street. Make me sensitive to the prompting of your Spirit, so that I can pray without ceasing for those who need it. In addition, by doing so, may I learn more about myself and hear your voice more clearly.

Week Six: Holy Spirit, fall on me anew this week in a powerful way. Fill me to overflowing, Spirit of Truth, my Counselor and Comforter. Anoint me with your power so I can be a bold witness for you and share the Good News of the resurrection with whomever you place in my path. Open up doors for me to give my testimony with others and to lovingly share the gospel of Christ with as many people as possible during this week before Easter.

Holy Week: Dearest Jesus, my Lord and Savior, this is the week you laid down your life for all humanity. You sacrificed everything for me because you loved me. Show me how I can make sacrifices in my life for you. Not to earn your favor, nor to receive your blessings, but simply to show how much I love you. Take from me whatever you might want to take because I am yours. Help me to realize exactly how much you gave up by dying on the cross. And help me, from this point onward, to let go of whatever I might be holding in my hands that is preventing me from fulfilling *your* desires and *your* purposes for my life.

Making Amends

Penance and Penitence

The sin of the individual member always in some measure infects the whole body. Therefore, during Lent and on the Fridays of the year, we do penance, not only on our own account, but also in the name of the Church and of the world. We must take very seriously our penitential obligations and be sure to carry them out.

Cardinal George Pell
Archbishop of Sydney
Sydney, Australia

Within the Roman Catholic Church and Eastern Orthodox Church, penance is an indispensable part of Lent. Penance, in fact, is considered a "sacrament," or a vehicle through which God imparts grace to the believer. According to the doctrine of penance, if someone is truly repentant (in other words, sorry for their sins), then they will not only feel remorse inwardly, but will desire to express that remorse outwardly by doing something commensurate with the sin's severity and the degree of regret they feel.

In his 2005 statement on "Lenten Penance," Cardinal George Pell, the Archbishop of Sydney, explained that penance (either a certain prayer, some specific act of charity, or good work like feeding the poor) is the "concrete expression of repentance. . . . [b]y penance we make satisfaction for our sins, and take real steps in the renewal of our lives." This is essentially proof of one's repentance, "a sign of the personal commitment that the Christian has made at this moment to begin—with the help of God—a new life in God's grace."

Protestants hold a different view on what constitutes proof of one's sorrow over sins. They preach *penitence* (penitence = repentance + penance). This is very similar to Roman Catholic penance in that it demonstrates one's anguish over having sinned, but there are two key differences: (1) whatever acts are done to show one's sorrow over sins are done at the individual's discretion (rather than at the instruction of a priest/church); and (2) whatever good deeds are done because of one's sorrow are not distinct from the repentance expressed. The inner repentance and its outward expression are considered the same thing.

Whether Roman Catholic or Protestant, believers have the same goal during Lent: "altering one's mind-set toward whole new ways of thinking and acting. . . . [T]aking a look at where we are and trying to see where we ought to be. . . . [T]esting our values and discerning how they stack up against the values that Jesus offers his followers" (The Reverend Daniel E. Pilarczyk, in "Lent: More Than Penance," *American Catholic*, www.americancatholic.org). This is accomplished to a great degree not only by repenting of sins, but also by showing that repentance outwardly.

Doing Good

Read the Instruction Manual

"Is not this the kind of fasting I have chosen: to loose the chains of injustice and untie the cords of the yoke, to set the oppressed free and break every yoke? Is it not to share your food with the hungry and to provide the poor wanderer with shelter—when you see the naked, to clothe him, and not turn away from your own flesh and blood?

Isaiah 58:6–7 NIV

Acts of Charity, also known as Good Works, play an equally vital role in the spiritual renewal that Christians seek during Lent. Donating goods or money to the poor, nursing the sick, visiting those imprisoned, sheltering the homeless, helping victims of natural disasters, and volunteering for church work all qualify as Good Works.

Such activities are clearly in line with Scripture. Moreover, the Bible tells us we were created for this. "For we are God's workmanship, created in Christ Jesus to do good works, which God prepared in advance for us to do" (Ephesians 2:10 NIV).

The purpose of doing Good Works during Lent, however, goes far beyond simply being nice. Each "good deed," so to speak, is to serve as a reminder to us of how we should *always* live, throughout the year, in obedience to Jesus' commands to "Love your neighbor as yourself" (Mark 12:31 NIV) and "do to others what you would have them do to you" (Matthew 7:12 NIV).

For those who have strayed from these instructions, Lent provides a wonderful way to get back on track and live righteously with compassion. Our acts of charity "make Christ's love present" to those whose lives we touch, said Pope John Paul II in his Lenten message for 2000.

Interestingly, in some Christian denominations, Good Works for Lent extend beyond such material assistance as making monetary contributions to the needy. *Spiritual* acts are acceptable as well, in the form of acts of penance/penitence. These Spiritual Works of Mercy, according to the United States Conference of Catholic Bishops, include: converting sinners, instructing the ignorant, advising the doubtful, comforting the sorrowful, bearing wrongs patiently, forgiving injuries, and praying for others.

Week Two

AT THE CROSS

Tearing Down Walls

Why Do We Need Saving?

But God demonstrates his own love for us in this: While we were still sinners, Christ died for us.

Romans 5:8 NIV

One question many people ask at Easter is *why* anyone needs to be saved. The answer can be summed up in one sentence: Because sin erected a wall of separation between humanity and God. "But your iniquities have separated you from your God; your sins have hidden his face from you, so that he will not hear" (Isaiah 59:2 NIV).

Obviously, to gain access to God, that wall needed to be broken down. According to the Bible, it is through Christ's death, that the wall of separation has been removed. "God was reconciling the world to himself in Christ, not counting men's sins against them. And he has committed to us the message of reconciliation" (2 Corinthians 5:19 NIV). As a result, we are reconciled to God, and have free access to him.

We are reconciled to God through Jesus' death. Such is the meaning behind the lyrics, "Peace on earth and mercy mild, God and sinners reconciled," in the famous Christmas carol "Hark! The Herald Angels Sing."

This means that reconciliation is not something we must accomplish ourselves. God does it *for* us. He has essentially thrown his arms open and said, *Everything standing between us has been removed. We are now reconciled in my eyes. Now it is up to you to either receive or reject the reconciliation by accepting Jesus as your savior.*

Each person can choose to take advantage of this free reconciliation. For those who do, complete forgiveness awaits them. It is one of the most precious gifts that God has made available to us through Christ's sacrifice on the cross.

The Perfect Gift

Simple Grace

Amazing grace! (how sweet the sound)
That sav'd a wretch like me!
I once was lost, but now am found,
Was blind, but now I see.

John Newton
1725–1807
Anglican clergyman

It must never be forgotten that salvation is a free gift. Nothing you do can earn a righteous position before God. As sinful human beings, all of us are unrighteous and always will be, left to ourselves. Yet God, by his grace, showed mercy by choosing to apply to us the righteousness of Christ when we accept by faith his death on the cross for us.

The Bible clearly states that we are justified apart from Good Works (or good behavior) and also apart from the law. "But now a righteousness from God, apart from law, has been made known, to which the Law and the Prophets testify. This righteousness from God comes through faith in Jesus Christ to all who believe. There is no difference" (Romans 3:21–22 NIV). "For it is by grace you have been saved, through faith—and this not from yourselves, it is the gift of God—not by works, so that no one can boast" (Ephesians 2:8–9 NIV).

God's affirmation of our righteous standing before him is similar to the legal declaration of the Supreme Court of the United States giving its final verdict. The case has been decided. We are innocent and righteous based on *Christ's* innocence and righteousness. The prosecution can make no further appeals nor take further actions.

This means that it is not even our faith that *earns* us salvation. Faith is merely the channel through which God's grace comes to the sinner.

A good illustration of how faith is involved in salvation comes with Christmas. Every year, we buy gifts for friends and relatives. Even before those gifts are received, they already belong to the recipients, wrapped, and waiting under the tree to bring joy. One need only accept and open the gift. In a similar way, sinners need only receive the gift of salvation to enjoy its glorious blessings.

Faith, therefore, is merely an attitude on which God acts. By faith a person is simply saying, "Yes, I believe you have a gift for me and I accept it." The gift, of course, was bought with Christ's own blood on the cross. "In him we have redemption through his blood, the forgiveness of sins, in accordance with the riches of God's grace that he lavished on us with all wisdom and understanding" (Ephesians 1:7–8 NIV).

But his death would have meant nothing if it had not been for the magnificent event that occurred three days after Jesus' crucifixion—his resurrection.

Morning by Morning

Nature's Themes

"There is no tale ever told that men would rather find was true, and none which so many skeptical men have accepted as true on its own merits."

J.R.R. Tolkien
1892–1973
Christian fantasy author

The concept of *resurrection* has been an integral part of human thought and religious belief since the dawn of time. The seasons of the year, for instance, were long ago tied to agricultural cycles and directed the thoughts of our ancestors toward the idea of resurrection. The withering of plant life in winter, along with the waning of the sun's heat and light, exemplified death. But when spring arrived, the sun once more burned brightly, giving its warmth to the barren world. The flowers and trees bloomed, and life was renewed.

Ancient peoples watched a similar cycle each day in the rising and setting of the sun. For untold centuries, many nations and tribes believed that the sun was nothing less than a god who died each evening and was reborn the next morning. Stars, too, underwent a kind of death and resurrection, but in reverse—twinkling to life at night, only to disappear during the waking hours, and then reappear after sunset.

Each person's encounter with sleep was seen as an illustration of life and death as well. In the ancient world, people thought of our nightly slumber as a kind of descent into the netherworld; when the senses shut down and the mind wandered away, no longer tethered to the earth.

We even get our English word "cemetery"

from a common Greek term (*koimeteron*) meaning a "rest house," or more specifically, "the sleeping place." This is how the word "sleep" became a metaphor for death. Such imagery turns up repeatedly in the Bible, for example, in Daniel 12:2: "Multitudes who sleep in the dust of the earth will awake: some to everlasting life, others to shame and everlasting contempt" (NIV).

Resurrection also entered the collective psyche of humankind, as people began to contemplate the good and bad fortunes of their society. During an epoch when communities were far more fragile than they are today, an entire tribe/nation might suffer widespread "death" via a lost battle, the plague, or some natural disaster. In time, the same community would experience resurrection through peace, health, and plenty, renewed to life and vitality.

People even associated their own emotional moods, either positive or negative, with life and death. According to Leon McKenzie, Professor Emeritus at Indiana University, the "taste of renewal" that came from exchanging a sad mood for a glad mood was compared to "a sense of deliverance" from the grave. The constant up-and-down swings of feelings, due to life's trials and tribulations, was seen as life, death, and then life again—resurrection.

Images of life arising out of death date to the very beginnings of history. Together they formed a kind of widespread resurrection motif that, in turn, gave birth to innumerable resurrection myths throughout different cultures across the aeons of time. Such myths invariably spoke of a dying and rising god-man, or a savior-hero, sent to rescue his people from their pain and struggles.

Here we have one of the most fascinating aspects of the resurrection story—its appearance in varying myth forms *before* Jesus Christ. How could this possibly be?

The incomparable Christian fantasy author J.R.R. Tolkien believed that all types of mythology existed as shadows of Christianity. According to one of his letters, he was not in the least bit shocked that other cultures far removed from the story of Christ would have created Christ-like myths:

> [L]egends and myths are largely made of "truth," and indeed present aspects of it that can only be received in this mode; and long ago certain truths and modes of this kind were discovered and must always reappear.

The great Christian apologist C. S. Lewis agreed, and like Tolkien, felt that the gospel stories themselves presented the greatest myth of all—the one that actually became fact! In Lewis' words, the narratives about Christ's life, death, and resurrection represent a "true myth, a myth that works on us in the same way as the others, but a myth that *really* happened." Tolkien, in *Tree and Leaf*, made a similar observation about the gospels:

> [They contain] many marvels—peculiarly artistic, beautiful, and moving: "mythical" in their perfect self-contained significance. . . . There is no tale ever told that men would rather find was true, and none which so many skeptical men have accepted as true on its own merits. For the Art of it has the supremely convincing tone of Primary Art, that is, of Creation. *Tree and Leaf.*

Tolkien and Lewis were two of the most respected Christian thinkers of the twentieth century. And for them, notes C. N. Manlove in *Modern Fantasy*, the gospel story constituted "the perfect fairy-tale [or myth] by the most potent of all authors—God himself."

For This Purpose He Came

The Meaning of Atonement

Grace and peace to you from God our Father and the Lord Jesus Christ, who gave himself for our sins to rescue us from the present evil age, according to the will of our God and Father.

Galations 1:3–4 NIV

Even while he was with them on earth, none of Christ's disciples understood why their beloved Lord had to die. Peter, in fact, went so far as to strenuously object to what Jesus had explained to them. "Never, Lord!" he said. "This shall never happen to you!" (Matthew 16:22 NIV).

Jesus, however, knew that he had come to earth to save sinners by sacrificing his life for them (1 Timothy 1:15 NIV) and through his death on the cross, "give his life as a ransom for many" (Matthew 20:28 NIV). "He himself bore our sins in his body on the tree, so that we might die to sins and live for righteousness; by his wounds you have been healed" (1 Peter 2:24 NIV).

This teaching about Jesus' death on behalf of sinners so that they might enjoy eternal life in the loving presence of God—known in Christianity as the doctrine of the atonement, or as some have phrased it, the "at-one-ment" of man and God—is the restoration of peace between sinful humanity and a holy God.

What exactly does "atonement" mean? Technically speaking, the word simply means a bringing together of estranged persons. When used in a theological sense, however, it refers to Christ's death, which healed God's estrangement from humanity.

The most common term the Bible uses in reference to Jesus' death for sinners is *substitution*. Christ, in other words, literally died in our place. This idea is expressed in dozens of biblical passages including this one, as rendered in the New Living Translation: "For God made Christ, who never sinned, to be the offering for our sin, so that we could be made right with God through Christ" (2 Corinthians 5:21). Theologian George Eldon Ladd explains further:

> In the death of Christ I died; I experienced the doom of sin; everything that the guilt of sin merits from the wrath of God was fulfilled in the death I died in Christ. . . . He died not only as my representative; he died in my stead, for it is because of his death that I shall be spared that death.

Jesus took the place of sinners, and in doing so, had their guilt and punishment transferred to him. He bore the punishment we rightly deserved for wrongs committed. He voluntarily "gave himself up for us as a fragrant offering and sacrifice to God" (Ephesians 5:2 NIV).

God can now show mercy toward us who have accepted Christ's substitution. His anger toward sin has been placated. *The Moody Handbook of Theology,* by Paul Enns, explains concisely:

> Because God is holy and righteous He cannot overlook sin; through the work of Jesus Christ, God is fully satisfied that His righteous standard has been met. Through union with Christ the believer can now be accepted by God and be spared from the wrath of God.

The punishment that Christ bore for us was necessary because any other method for removing our sins would have run contrary to God's just, holy, and perfect nature, which demands that sin be punished. Christ not only saved us, but also demonstrated the righteousness of God to the world "God presented him as a sacrifice of atonement, through faith in his blood.

"He did this to demonstrate his justice, because in his forebearance he had left the sins committed beforehand unpunished—he did it to demonstrate his justice at the present time, so as to be just and the one who justifies those who have faith in Jesus" (Romans 3:25–26 NIV).

Jesus himself taught, "This is my blood of the covenant, which is poured out for many for the forgiveness of sins" (Matthew 26:28 NIV).

This is not to say that there was some magical power in Christ's physical blood that literally washed away sins, as water washes away dirt. As R. C. Sproul remarked many years ago in his popular daily Bible study guide, *Table Talk,* "[i]f Jesus had cut his finger in Joseph's carpentry workshop, it would have had no redemptive significance." In other words, the biblical references to Christ shedding his blood are metaphorical references to his death.

You Were a Slave

A Ransom Paid for Us

You were bought at a price; do not become slaves of men.

1 Corinthians 7:23 NIV

Redemption, another belief wrapped up in the atonement, comes from the Hebrew words *padah* (to redeem) and *ga'al* (to ransom).

Padah, according to the *Expository Dictionary of Bible Words,* "was originally used commercially to indicate a transfer of ownership." It appears in several Old Testament verses that speak of God's ownership of the people whom he rescued out of Egypt. "Remember that you were slaves in Egypt and that the Lord your God brought you out of there with a mighty hand and an outstretched arm. Therefore the Lord your God has commanded you to observe the Sabbath day" (Deuteronomy 5:15 NIV).

The *Expository Dictionary of Bible Words* further explains that *ga'al* has a similar meaning to *padah*, but points more precisely to someone who plays "the part of a kinsman, that is, to act on behalf of a relative in trouble or danger."

Both *ga'al* and *padah* refer to persons or objects, which although owned by an individual, are under the power/control of another person. The words also indicate that the true owner is unable to secure the release of his or her possessions until a third party intervenes.

These terms provide great insight into how Christ redeemed sinners through a payment of debt; especially when considered in light of the three Greek words found in the

New Testament that are most often applied to what Jesus did on the cross.

First, we have the word *agorazo,* translated as "bought," that was used in Greek culture to describe the purchase of slaves. "You were bought at a price. Therefore honor God with your body" (1 Corinthians 6:20 NIV). *The Moody Handbook of Theology* tells us that in the Bible this word connotes, "the believer being purchased out of the slave market of sin and set free from sin's bondage through the death of Jesus Christ."

Revelation 14:4 reads: "These are those who did not defile themselves with women, for they kept themselves pure. They follow the Lamb wherever he goes. They were purchased from among men and offered as first fruits to God and the Lamb" (NIV).

Next, there is *exagorazo,* a strengthened form of *agorazo.* It also means "to buy out," and like *agorazo,* is commonly linked to the purchasing of slaves, but with a view to their freedom and focuses more on the actual price paid, explains *Vine's Complete Expository Dictionary of Old and New Testament Words*.

The apostle Paul uses it in reference to Christ's deliverance of the Jews from the law and its curse. "Christ redeemed us from the curse of the law by becoming a curse for us, for it is written: 'Cursed is everyone who is hung on a tree'" (Galatians 3:13 NIV).

Finally, *lutroo* means "to obtain release by the payment of a price," as defined in Fritz Rienecker's *A Linguistic Key to the Greek New Testament*. It conveys the notion of being set free through a ransom. "But we had hoped that he was the one who was going to redeem Israel" (Luke 24:21 NIV).

Christians have been literally purchased by the blood of Jesus Christ (his death), said the apostle Peter. "It was not with perishable things . . . that you were redeemed from the empty way of life handed down to you from your forefathers, but with the precious blood of Christ, a lamb without blemish or defect" (1 Peter 1:18–19 NIV). Unlike both of the other Greek words, according to Vine, *lutroo* emphasizes the exact event of deliverance itself or the act of setting someone free.

An Extension of Credit

Beyond Mere Forgiveness

Since we have now been justified by his blood, how much more shall we be saved from God's wrath through him!

Romans 5:9 NIV

With forgiveness alone, all Christians would simply be forgiven sinners who still did not possess the absolute righteousness (moral perfection) to enter God's kingdom. Righteousness is something entirely different, it must be given to us via justification.

Forgiveness merely *removes* something (sin and its penalty), while justification *imparts* something (a righteous standing before God). This is why forgiveness has often been termed the "negative" side of atonement, while justification is its "positive" side. Of course, the most important aspect of both forgiveness and justification is that we obtain them by grace through faith alone.

Justification is the act whereby God once and for all declares someone "righteous":

> However, to the man who does not work but trusts God who justifies the wicked, his faith is credited as righteousness. . . . "Blessed are they whose transgressions are forgiven, whose sins are covered. Blessed is the man whose sin the Lord will never count against him." (Romans 4:5–8 NIV)

This happens as a direct result of God's grace, or unmerited favor, toward anyone who accepts by faith the saving power of Jesus' work on the cross. Christ's righteousness is credited to us as if we ourselves were righteous. We can actually claim his righteousness as our own. Justification is not only the pinnacle of what Christ did for us, but also the unavoidable prerequisite for entering heaven.

Simply put, without justification we would not be able stand in God's presence—even though forgiven of our sins.

Reaping the Harvest
The Idea of Resurrection

So will it be with the resurrection of the dead.
1 Corinthians 15:42 NIV

During Jesus' ministry, *resurrection* was a familiar theme. Every culture, as we previously discovered in our last chapter, had witnessed it on a yearly, monthly, and daily basis. Even the famous French philosopher Voltaire, although not a Christian, recognized that "everything in nature is resurrection."

In other words, the idea of returning to life after death was something that creation itself had been depicting for countless ages. So it makes sense that God would use such an event to save his people. He often used familiar themes, well-known symbols, and simple stories to teach great truths.

In the ancient world, for example, the harvest was viewed as a kind of resurrection. Seeds planted in the dirt, or buried in death, sprang to life many months later. They were reborn as something new, and yet were connected in a dramatic way to their previous forms. An obvious question arose: Might this not be possible for friends and relatives who had passed away?

The apostle Paul, interestingly, used this very image in 1 Corinthians 15:35–44 to explain the Christian's hope of resurrection:

> But someone may ask, "How are the dead raised? With what kind of body will they come?" How foolish! What you sow does not come to life unless it dies. When you sow, you do not plant the body that will be, but just a seed, perhaps of

wheat or of something else. But God gives it a body as he has determined. . . . So will it be with the resurrection of the dead. The body that is sown is perishable, it is raised imperishable; it is sown in dishonor, it is raised in glory; it is sown in weakness, it is raised in power; it is sown a natural body, it is raised a spiritual body. (NIV)

Week Three

REASONS TO BELIEVE

Skeptics among Us

Jesus Said It, We Believe It

The whole preaching thrust of the apostolic age was based upon the fact that one quiet morning in an obscure garden, man had vanquished his most feared enemy, the vaunted dark angel of death.

Walter Martin
1928–1989
Christian theologian and author
From *Essential Christianity*

Does it really matter whether Jesus *literally* rose from the dead? Not according to some people. For instance, Ronald Gregor Smith, the author of *Secular Christianity* writes, "We may freely say that the bones of Jesus lie somewhere in Palestine. Christian faith is not destroyed by this admission."

The Bible, however, disagrees, stating

matter-of-factly, that the reality of Jesus' resurrection is vital to the entire Christian belief system: "And if Christ has not been raised, your faith is futile; you are still in your sins!" (1 Corinthians 15:17 NIV).

The resurrection also reflects on Jesus' character, trustworthiness, and integrity, since he explicitly predicted that he would rise from the dead three days after his crucifixion, according to various passages recorded in Matthew, Mark, Luke and John.

For example, Matthew 16:20–21 says, "Then he warned his disciples not to tell anyone that he was Christ. From that time on Jesus began to explain to his disciples that he must go to Jerusalem and suffer many things at the hands of the elders, the chief priests and the teachers of the law, and that he must be killed and on the third day be raised to life" (NIV).

If Jesus did not *literally* rise from the

grave, then he was either a deceiver or a lunatic. There are no other options. He could not have simply been a "good teacher" who made false prophecies and errors about his own life and death.

Furthermore, the truthfulness of Christ's resurrection is significant for the future state of the world and all humanity. The visible power manifested by God in Jesus' resurrection provides assurance of humankind's final judgment. "For he has set a day when he will judge the world with justice by the man he has appointed. He has given proof of this to everyone by raising him from the dead" (Acts 17:31 NIV).

Moreover, Christ is called the "firstfruits of those who have fallen asleep" (1 Corinthians 15:20 NIV) and the "firstborn from (among) the dead" (Colossians 1:18; Revelation 1:5 NIV). Jesus' resurrection, simply put, is a kind of picture of what will happen to believers.

"It symbolized what was destined to happen to the members of Christ's mystical body in their justification, spiritual birth, and future blessed resurrection," wrote Louis Berkhof in his *Systematic Theology.*

Sadly, the Easter season always seems to bring out those seeking to cast doubt on the validity of the resurrection. A few of their skeptical explanations at first may seem plausible, but upon careful examination, we can dismiss them with confidence in favor of a truth that is not only more marvelous, but also more probable—that Christ, in fact, did rise bodily from the grave.

Some people, for instance, allege that the accounts of Christ's post-crucifixion appearances were nothing more than fictitious additions to the gospels, which were themselves supposedly written hundreds of years after the fact to legitimize Christianity.

Others say that Jesus may have come out of the grave, but only after he was "revived" from a fainting spell (in other words, he never really died).

Additional critics allege that Christ did indeed die, but that the apostles, rather than admit that their Messiah was dead, conspired to steal the body and lie about Christ's resurrection.

A few individuals have actually gone so far as to assert that Jesus himself tried to deceive everyone by faking his death, but *accidentally* died. Later, they say, an impostor "appeared" to the faithful and claimed that he was the risen Christ!

Finally, there are those who believe Christ rose from the dead, but only as a spirit.

Regarding the accusations against the gospels themselves, there is no proof that the resurrection accounts were fraudulent additions to the original texts. The biblical manuscripts still in existence read extraordinarily similar. Moreover, the gospels were in reality written very close to the time of

Jesus' death and resurrection. They were *not* transcribed hundreds of years later. All of them were composed before 70 AD, and perhaps as early as the 50s AD.

The other so-called explanations of the resurrection also fail to accurately reflect either the biblical records or the historical data, and can be easily refuted, as we shall now see.

Did He Fake It?

The Jesus-Fainted Version

Were you there when they laid him in the tomb?

From an African-American spiritual

One of the most popular secular notions disputing the resurrection is the "swoon theory"—that Jesus didn't die on the cross, but merely fainted. This loss of consciousness supposedly prompted onlookers to mistakenly believe that he had expired. Those present at his crucifixion then took Christ down from the cross and prematurely placed him in a tomb. There, the spices that anointed his body and the cool air of the grave revived our Lord, thus enabling him to roll back the stone of the tomb three days later and emerge refreshed (despite the fact that he wouldn't have had anything to eat or drink for three days).

This hypothesis is riddled with improbabilities and speculation that render it beyond acceptance. John 19:31–42 (NIV) gives this account of the moments just after Jesus died on the cross:

> Because the Jews did not want the bodies left on the crosses during the Sabbath, they asked Pilate to have the legs broken and the bodies taken down. The soldiers therefore came and broke the legs of the first man who had been crucified with Jesus, and then those of the other. But when they came to Jesus and found that he was already dead, they did not break his legs. Instead, one of the soldiers pierced Jesus' side with a spear, bringing a sudden flow of blood and water.

The man who saw it has given testimony, and his testimony is true. He knows that he tells the truth, and he testifies so that you also may believe. These things happened so that the scripture would be fulfilled: "Not one of his bones will be broken," and, as another scripture says, "They will look on the one they have pierced."

Later, Joseph of Arimathea asked Pilate for the body of Jesus. Now Joseph was a disciple of Jesus, but secretly because he feared the Jews. With Pilate's permission, he came and took the body away. He was accompanied by Nicodemus, the man who earlier had visited Jesus at night. Taking Jesus' body, the two of them wrapped it, with the spices, in strips of linen. This was in accordance with Jewish burial customs.

At the place where Jesus was crucified,

> there was a garden, and in the garden a new tomb, in which no one had ever been laid. Because it was the Jewish day of Preparation and since the tomb was nearby, they laid Jesus there.

In their *Handbook of Christian Apologetics*, Peter Kreeft and Ronald K. Tacelli demonstrated nine logical flaws inherent to the swoon theory:

1. Jesus could not have survived crucifixion. Roman procedures were very careful to eliminate that possibility. Roman law even laid the death penalty on any soldier who let a capital prisoner escape in any way, including bungling a crucifixion. . . .
2. The fact that the Roman soldier did not break Jesus' legs, as he did the other two crucified criminals (John 19:31–33), means that the soldier was sure Jesus was dead. . . .

3. John, an eyewitness, certified that he saw blood and water come from Jesus' pierced heart (John 19:34–35). This shows that Jesus' lungs had collapsed and he had died of asphyxiation. Any medical expert can vouch for this.
4. The body was totally encased in winding sheets and entombed (John 19:38–42).
5. The post-resurrection appearances convinced the disciples, even "doubting Thomas," that Jesus was gloriously alive. . . . A half-dead, staggering sick man who has just had a narrow escape is not worshiped fearlessly as divine lord and conqueror of death. "That evening, on the first day of the week, the disciples were meeting behind locked doors because they were afraid of the Jewish leaders. Suddenly, Jesus was standing there among them! 'Peace be with you,' he said. As he spoke, he held out his hands for them to see, and

he showed them his side. They were filled with joy when they saw their Lord! . . . Then Jesus told him [Thomas], 'You believe because you have seen me. Blessed are those who haven't seen me and believe anyway' " (John 20:19–29).

6. How were the Roman guards at the tomb overpowered by a swooning corpse? Or by unarmed apostles?
7. How would a swooning half-dead man have moved a great stone at the door of the tomb? Who moved the stone if not an angel?
8. If Jesus awoke from a swoon, where did he go? . . . A man like that, with a past like that, would have left traces.
9. Most simply, the swoon theory necessarily turns into the conspiracy theory or the hallucination theory [that is, everyone merely *thought* they saw Jesus die], for the disciples testified that Jesus did not swoon but really died.

Clearly, the swoon theory is untenable. Even liberal scholars of the nineteenth century discounted it, including David Strauss, the author of *New Life of Jesus,* and Ian Wilson, who penned *Jesus: The Evidence.*

Modern medicine, too, has dismissed the theory. A March 21, 1986, article that appeared in *The Journal of the American Medical Society* concluded the following:

> [T]he weight of historical evidence and medical evidence indicates that Jesus was dead before the wound to his side was inflicted and supports the traditional view that the spear, thrust between his right ribs, probably perforated not only the right lung but also the pericardium and heart and thereby ensured his death. Accordingly, interpretations based on the assumption that Jesus did not die on the cross appear to be at odds with modern medical knowledge.

It seems, then, that Jesus truly died, and that he was laid in the tomb, bound in long strips of fabric just as any other deceased person of that era would have been buried.

A Conspiracy Theory

Apostles Accused of Grave Robbing

Jesus answered them, "Destroy this temple, and I will raise it again in three days" . . . After he was raised from the dead, his disciples recalled what he had said. Then they believed the Scripture and the words that Jesus had spoken.

John 2:19–22 NIV

What of the conspiracy theory involving some unnamed disciples carrying away their teacher's body? Could this not be the answer to the empty tomb? Definitely not.

According to the resurrection conspiracy theory, as explained by Louis Berkhof in his *Systematic Theology,* the apostles "practiced deliberate deception by stealing the body from the grave and then declaring the Lord had risen." This allegation comes directly from the original fabrication spread by the religious authorities of the day soon after the discovery that Jesus had risen from the dead:

> While the women were on their way, some of the guards went into the city and reported to the chief priests everything that had happened. When the chief priests had met with the elders and devised a plan, they gave the soldiers a large sum of money, telling them, "You are to say, 'His disciples came during the night and stole him away while we were asleep.' If this report gets to the governor we will satisfy him and keep you out of trouble." So the soldiers took the money and did as they were instructed. And this story has been widely circulated among the Jews to this very day. (Matthew 28:11–15 NIV)

A problematic question immediately springs to mind: What would the disciples have gained by perpetrating such a hoax? History reveals that Christ's followers lost everything, including their lives, because they preached their risen Lord. It is highly improbable that the apostles would have allowed themselves and their families to suffer excruciating torment and death to advance what they *knew* to be a lie.

Advocates of the conspiracy theory also run into a serious logistic problem—the Roman soldiers who were guarding the tomb. How would a ragtag group of frightened, disorganized fishermen overcome trained Roman warriors to steal a body?

It is doubtful that the soldiers would have fallen asleep on the job, knowing that such a failure would have meant their execution. Even if they had dozed off momentarily, "the crowd and the effort and the noise it would have taken to move an enormous boulder would have awakened them," notes Kreeft and Tacelli in their *Handbook of Christian Apologetics*.

Finally, throughout early church history, we have no Christian ever confessing "freely or under pressure, bribe, or even torture, that the whole story of the resurrection was a fake, a lie, a deliberate deception," add Kreeft and Tacelli.

Even when people denied their faith under torture and worshiped Caesar, they *never* said that the resurrection was a conspiracy. It is only reasonable to assume that out of the thousands of poor souls tortured for Christ, at least one person would have revealed that the whole resurrection was a concocted tale—if that had been the case.

No such confession was ever reported.

The Jesus Impersonator?

Rumors, Rumors

So the women hurried away from the tomb, afraid yet filled with joy, and ran to tell his disciples. Suddenly Jesus met them. "Greetings," he said. They came to him, clasped his feet and worshiped him. Then Jesus said to them, "Do not be afraid. Go and tell my brothers to go to Galilee; there they will see me."

Matthew 28:8–10 NIV

Another speculation about the resurrection that is similar to, but slightly different from, the conspiracy theory is the "Passover Plot" (or the impostor theory). Its scenario is even more improbable because it impugns the integrity and honesty not only of the apostles, but also of Christ himself. The theory was originally advanced in the 1965 book *The Passover Plot,* by Hugh J. Schonfield. He claimed that after Jesus' death, Joseph of Arimathea, Lazarus, and a mysterious "young man" conspired with Jesus to fool the other disciples into thinking that Jesus was the Messiah.

The plan called for Christ to ingest a drug that would enable him to fake his death. Afterward, he would be revived by his cohorts and emerge from the tomb as the risen Messiah! Unfortunately, so the plot goes, the crucifixion wounds—including the gash in Christ's side from the spear—proved fatal.

The remaining plotters salvaged their plan by stealing Christ's body and then having the "young man" appear throughout Galilee as Jesus. In other words, all of the encounters "Christ" had with eyewitnesses to his resurrection were cases of mistaken identity.

Obviously, there are numerous difficulties with this tall tale. First, a dishonest plot doesn't coincide with the character and personality that Jesus consistently displayed throughout his life.

Second, no person(s) could have orchestrated the number of Old Testament prophecies fulfilled in Jesus' life including when, where, how, from what tribe, and during which dynasty Christ would come. For example, in Micah 5:2, we read, "But you, Bethlehem Ephrathah, though you are small among the clans of Judah, out of you will come for me one who will be ruler over Israel, whose origins are from of old, from ancient times" (NIV).

Third, too many people intimately acquainted with Jesus saw him after the resurrection (close friends, followers, and family members). It would have been impossible for all of them to be mistaken about his identity.

As with all of the alternate explanations of the resurrection, the "Passover Plot" fails to tarnish the bold testimony that Christ's followers have been declaring at Easter for over 2,000 years: He is risen!

More Than a Spirit

Seeing Him as Flesh and Blood

He was not seen by all the people, but by witnesses whom God had already chosen—by us who ate and drank with him after he rose from the dead.

Acts 10:41 NIV

Many different religious groups throughout the world accept the notion that Christ rose from the dead as a spirit only. Scripture, however, indicates quite plainly that the body that hung on the cross, and the one that went into the grave, was the same body that rose and came out of the tomb. Jesus, for instance, was touched and handled by his followers after rising to life: "Reach out your hand and put it into my side. Stop doubting and believe" (John 20:27 NIV).

After his resurrection, Jesus also ate food to prove that he was physically present. "And while they still did not believe it because of joy and amazement, he asked them, 'Do you have anything here to eat?' They gave him a piece of broiled fish, and he took it and ate it in their presence" (Luke 24:41–43 NIV). He said himself that he possessed flesh and bones, going so far as to make it clear that "a ghost does not have flesh and bones" (Luke 24:39 NIV).

Another noteworthy statement from Jesus appears in John 2:19 where, in reference to his body, he proclaims: "Destroy this temple, and I will raise it again in three days" (NIV).

Notice how Christ said destroy "*this* temple [meaning his body] . . . and I will raise *it* [the same one] again." He didn't say, "Destroy this temple and I will raise another one again in three days." Either Jesus did what he said he would do or he didn't.

At first his followers failed to understand the meaning behind these words. But the apostle John explains: "The temple he had spoken of was his body. After he rose from the dead, his disciples recalled what he had said. Then they believed the Scripture and the words that Jesus had spoken" (John 2:21–22 NIV).

Also, the Greek word used by John to clarify Christ's statement about his "body" (Greek, *soma,* v. 21) indicates that a fleshly body would rise up. The noun *soma,* a medical term, is always used in the New Testament for a physical body—never a spiritual one.

Finally, an extremely powerful verse in the Bible that shows the nature of Christ's resurrection body is Colossians 2:9, which declares "For in Christ all the fullness of the Deity lives in bodily form" (NIV). If Jesus was raised as a spirit, then how could this passage claim that deity is presently dwelling in

Christ's body? It couldn't. Obviously, according to Scripture, Christ was raised bodily from the grave.

So is it all just a matter of blind faith? Of course not. Faith certainly is an integral *part* of Christianity. After all, no one alive today was actually there when Jesus emerged from the tomb. And the New Testament does declare explicitly that without faith, it is "impossible" to please God (see Hebrews 11:6 NIV).

At the same time, however, God doesn't want us believing *blindly* in him. We need not accept anything that is either implausible or against reason. On the contrary, those who celebrate Christ's resurrection can enjoy a faith in him that is rooted and grounded in solid historical facts, rational thinking, and reasonable *conclusions* based on the evidence.

Our faith, as Christian philosophy professor Winfried Corduan has put it, is a reasonable faith.

A Skeptic Believes

The Journalist Who Examined Christianity

Now faith is being sure of what we hope for and certain of what we do not see.

Hebrews 11:1 NIV

The logical arguments for Jesus' resurrection are so substantial that they have "persuaded many skeptics who started to examine the evidence for the purpose of disproving the resurrection," asserts Wayne Grudem in his *Systematic Theology.*

Consider, for instance, the story of ex-skeptic and former legal editor for the *Chicago Tribune,* Lee Strobel. He lived as a hardcore atheist for many years, until he took the challenge to investigate Christianity using his journalistic training.

After two years, he concluded that the

evidence was overwhelming for the resurrection and accepted Christ as his savior. He eventually became a pastor, and has even written several books in a "Case for" series of volumes that not only chronicle his investigation, but also defend the various aspects of Christianity. They include *The Case for Christ* and *The Case for Faith*.

Strobel's experience is not unique. According to E. M. Blaiklock, historian and professor of classics at Auckland University, "[t]he evidence for the life, the death, and the resurrection of Christ is better authenticated than most of the facts of ancient history."

Professor Thomas Arnold, at one time the chair of modern history at Oxford, similarly remarked, "I know of no one fact in the history of mankind which is proved by better and fuller evidence of every sort, to the understanding of a fair inquirer, than the great sign which God hath given us that Christ died and rose again from the dead."

The Evidence Is In

But Can You Prove a Miracle?

It was Mary Magdalene, Joanna, and Mary the mother of James and the others with them told this to the apostles. But they did not believe the women because the words seemed to them like nonsense. Peter, however, got up and ran to the tomb.

Luke 24:10–12 NIV

The empty tomb in which Jesus' body had been is the first piece of evidence that, at the very least, suggests Christ rose from the dead. The religious leaders who had conspired to kill Jesus certainly knew that an empty tomb would be a powerful sign of his identity as Messiah. That is obvious given their request to have Roman guards placed at the tomb's entrance.

The chief priests and Pharisees had to

insure that no one would be able to steal the body. A missing corpse would go a long way toward validating Jesus' prediction about rising from the dead.

"So give the order for the tomb to be made secure until the third day. Otherwise, his disciples may come and steal the body and tell the people that he has been raised from the dead. This last deception will be worse than the first" (Matthew 27:64 NIV).

Despite the precautions, Christ's tomb was empty precisely when he said it would be. Witnesses to that miracle, as mentioned by the different gospel writers included: Mary Magdalene; the mother of James (also known as "the other Mary"); Salome; Joanna; an unspecified number of "other women"; Peter; and John.

Some non-Christians have argued that the empty tomb found by the all of these eyewitnesses was not actually Jesus' grave. Twentieth century liberal theologian Kirsopp Lake, for example, claimed that "in their grief the women lost their way, went to an empty tomb in the same general area where Jesus was buried, and jumped to the conclusion that Jesus had risen from the dead."

The problem with this theory, of course, is that Jesus was not laid in just any old tomb that happened to be nearby. Joseph of Arimathea—a prominent member of the Jewish Sanhedrin—the supreme council over religious, civil, and criminal matters in ancient Israel—graciously donated his tomb for Christ's internment. Joseph himself, along with the Pharisee Nicodemus, took Jesus' body to the gravesite (see John 19:38–42 NIV).

If the women had voiced any questions about the tomb's location, these men could easily have answered them. Besides, the women knew its exact location because they watched Joseph place Jesus' body in it, according to three other gospels. In Matthew's account, Joseph "rolled a big stone in front of the entrance to the tomb and went away. Mary Magdalene and the other Mary were sitting there opposite the tomb" (Matthew 27:60–61 NIV).

Of course, an empty tomb is not by itself conclusive proof that Jesus rose from the dead. Its import is greatly increased, however, by evidence of the post-resurrection appearances of Christ. These eyewitness accounts are extremely impressive.

The Bible mentions many people who observed, spoke to, and even ate with the resurrected Christ in numerous passages of the New Testament. They ranged from friends, to followers, to strangers, to relatives, to new converts: Mary Magdalene, several women, two disciples on the road to Emmaus; the apostles (minus Thomas) and many others in the upper room; the disciples (including Thomas); seven disciples fishing on the Sea of Galilee; all eleven disciples on a mountain in Galilee; the disciples in Jerusalem, more than five hundred brethren; James, Jesus' half brother. The disciples were also present when the Lord ascended into heaven:

> After his suffering, he showed himself to these men and gave many convincing proofs that he was alive. He appeared to them over a period of forty days and spoke about the kingdom of God. On one occasion, while he was eating with them, he gave them this command: "Do not leave Jerusalem, but wait for the gift my Father promised, which you have heard me speak about. For John baptized with water, but in a few days you will be baptized with the Holy Spirit."
>
> So when they met together, they asked him, "Lord, are you at this time going to restore the kingdom to Israel?"
>
> He said to them: "It is not for you to know the times or dates the Father has set by his own authority. But you will receive power when the Holy Spirit comes

> on you; and you will be my witnesses in Jerusalem, and in all Judea and Samaria, and to the ends of the earth."
>
> After he said this, he was taken up before their very eyes, and a cloud hid him from their sight. (Acts 1:3–9 NIV)

Those who dismiss these accounts claim that using biblical testimony in such a manner is circular reasoning, since the Bible is being used to prove the Bible. That would be a valid argument if the Bible were one book, but the New Testament is not one book written by one author. It is a *collection* of twenty-seven books by several authors. The witnesses to whom Christ appeared are mentioned in five different books penned by four different writers. Consequently, using the biblical texts to support the reality of the resurrection is not circular reasoning. It is an appeal to a variety of sources.

Week Four

The Meanings of Easter

Just the Facts

A Detail Here, a Detail There

On the first day of the week, very early in the morning, the women took the spices they had prepared and went to the tomb.

Luke 24:1 NIV

The complementary way that the gospel writers record the resurrection provides additional evidence pointing to the likelihood that Jesus rose from the dead. Their separate accounts serve to highlight diverse facets of the resurrection from alternative perspectives—exactly what one might expect from different authors describing a similar occurrence. This type of reporting is common in modern newspaper articles on a particular story or experience. The differences are *complementary,* not contradictory.

Consider, for example, the apparent contradiction between John 20:1 which says that Mary Magdalene went to the tomb "while it was still dark" (NIV) and Mark 16:1–2 which states that Mary Magdalene went to the tomb with other women "just after sunrise" (NIV). Did Mary go to the tomb alone, or was she accompanied by other women? Was it dark, or was it morning? On the surface, these may seem like difficult questions. In reality, we can answer them with relative ease.

John does not say that Mary traveled to the grave alone. He merely tells us a single fact from his perspective—that Mary went to the tomb. This is the only thing John wanted to communicate. Matthew, on the other hand, wanted to tell us more about what transpired. He provided complementary information so we would know Mary was not alone. Mark goes even further, revealing the other women's names. "When the Sabbath was over, Mary Magdalene, Mary the mother of James, and Salome bought spices so that they might go to anoint Jesus' body" (Mark 16:1 NIV). And in Luke 24:10 we are told "It was Mary Magdalene, Joanna, Mary the mother of James, and the others with them" (NIV).

As for the time of day, the Greek words used in all four gospels, taken together, establish a realistic picture of when and how long it took the women to walk from Jerusalem to the tomb. Gleason Archer concludes in his *Encyclopedia of Bible Difficulties*:

> They apparently started their journey from the house in Jerusalem when it was still dark (*skotias eti ouses*), even though it was already morning (*proi*) [John. 20:1]. . . . but by the time they arrived, dawn was glimmering in the east

> (*te epiphoskouse*) that Sunday morning (*eis mian sabbaton*) [Matt. 28:1]. . . . Mark [see Mark. 16-2 above] adds that the tip of the sun had actually appeared above the horizon (*anateilantos tou heliou. . .* .).

These are but a few examples of the complementary details existing in the gospels that add a measurable degree of believability to the story of Jesus. If the account were not true, then one might expect either a list of unsolvable contradictions, or a perfect duplication of text so rigid as to betray a deliberately concocted tale that had never truly taken place.

Instead, we have what Alister McGrath, a research lecturer in theology at Oxford University and theology professor at Regent College, characterizes as a story with variations on minor points of detail, which "is a characteristic feature of eyewitness reports."

Clearly, there exists a great deal of evidence to substantiate the resurrection of Jesus the Christ and ample reason to accept the event as historical fact. Because of our Lord's triumph over death, Christians can confidently echo the promise proclaimed to the world more than 2,000 years ago by Paul the apostle: "For he has set a day when he will judge the world with justice by the man he has appointed. He has given proof of this to all men by raising him from the dead" (Acts 17:31 NIV).

When Is Easter?

Setting a Date

This is a day you are to commemorate; for the generations to come you shall celebrate it as a festival to the Lord—a lasting ordinance.

Exodus 12:14 NIV

Having accepted the facts of Jesus' resurrection and its relevance to salvation, the followers of Christ eventually found ways to recall the miracles they had experienced. By a church decree passed in 325 AD, Easter became the Sunday after the first full moon following the *vernal equinox* (when the sun passes from the southern hemisphere into the northern hemisphere). Easter, however, soon became far more than just a single day of commemoration. Over the centuries, it evolved into an entire season of holy days or holidays created to highlight aspects of Jesus' life leading up to his resurrection.

No one knows precisely how, when, or where the Easter celebration started. Scholars of religion believe its observance probably has roots in the very earliest days of the church, when the majority of Christians were recent converts from Judaism. Consequently, the commemoration of Jesus' resurrection coincided for many years with the Jewish Passover, known as *Pesah* in Hebrew and *Pascha* in Greek.

Such a name was fitting, not only because Christ died and rose over the Passover memorial, but also because Passover itself had been instituted by the Israelites, as outlined in Exodus 12:1–29, as a foreshadowing of the Messiah, whose blood would have to be spilled so his people could be spared from death. However, once Christians felt the need to distance themselves from Judaism, they moved *Pascha* from Passover (the 14th of Nisan on the Jewish calendar) to dates that varied from location to location.

Finally, at the Council of Nicea in 325 AD, church leaders officially set the date as the Sunday after the first full moon following the vernal equinox. Despite this ruling, Easter continued to fall on varying days throughout the Christian world well into the sixteenth century because different calendars were in use. Even today, as much as five weeks may sometimes separate the Western church's celebration of Easter from its observance under the Eastern Orthodox Church's calendar.

Although the early church may have differed on the date for *Pascha*, the memorial itself looked strikingly similar throughout every Christian community. It was typically a single night honoring Christ's resurrection *and* his death. The believers prayed, read Scripture, lighted a "Paschal Candle," and received communion—also known as the taking of the Eucharist. Eventually, however, two celebrations emerged: one on Easter eve (Holy Saturday) and one on Easter morning (similar to today's sunrise ceremonies).

Spreading the Good News

Finding Common Ground

I have become all things to all men so that by all possible means I might save some.

1 Corinthians 9:22b

Christians, as far back as the first century, have faced a difficult task. On the one hand, Jesus commanded his followers to "preach the word" (2 Timothy 4:2 NIV), and always "be prepared to give an answer to everyone who asks you to give the reason for the hope that you have" (1 Peter 3:15 NIV).

On the other hand, the Lord also instructed believers in him to treat others respectfully, showing them kindness, honor, and love, as in 2 Timothy 2:24–25 (NIV)—even when it comes to any views that might contradict the Bible and the gospel message.

During the church's earliest years this immediately presented Christians with a fine line to walk, not only because they were, at that time, being persecuted by the Romans, but also because they were surrounded by a multitude of religions competing for converts; most notably, paganism. One of the ways believers attempted to obey scripture's two-fold admonition to preach the gospel with reverence and respect, was by using customs, symbols, language, and even quotations from pagan sources as witnessing tools.

For example, the apostles John and Paul saw that various pagan philosophers had actually made some rather astute observations about God that possessed truths consistent with Christianity. So when writing scripture, they used pagan concepts as a jumping-off point, so to speak, before sharing spiritual truths.

In John's gospel, for instance, the Greek word *Logos* ("Word") is used for Jesus. This word is a Greek philosophical term that in Christ's era represented "reason" as a bridge between the unreachable God and earthly matter. Hence, Jesus, as the eternal *Logos*, is the bridge between God and man.

Paul appealed even more to non-Christian sources. Consider his sermon to the Athenians in Acts 17:22–34, where he mentions their altar to "THE UNKNOWN GOD," saying, "What you worship as something unknown I am going to proclaim to you" (NIV). He concluded: "[God] is not far from each one of us (Acts 17:27 NIV). For in him we live and move, and have our being. As some of your own poets have said, 'We are also his offspring.'"

The words "we live and move and have our being" are from a poem by the pagan Epimenides of Crete (around 600 BC) to the Supreme God. And "For we are also his offspring" is from *Phenomena* by the pagan poet Aratus of Cilicia (third century BC)—it reflects the teachings of Cleanthes, a Greek Stoic philosopher (also third century BC). He also cited pagans in Titus 1:12, and in 1 Corinthians 15:33.

This tradition of borrowing pagan/non-Christian symbols, dates, celebrations, and imagery in an effort to refocus an unbelieving world's attention on Christ continued long after Paul and John died, and well into the establishment of the church.

The fish, for instance, which came to symbolize Christ, was originally used by pagans as a sign of their fish goddess, Themis. Likewise, we have wedding rings, an integral part of Christian weddings, but they too were initially pagan. And, of course, there is Easter.

Double Meanings

Pagan Imagery Put to Work for Christ

It was just before the Passover Feast. Jesus knew that the time had come for him to leave this world and go to the Father. Having loved his own who were in the world, he now showed them the full extent of his love.

John 13:1 NIV

The very name "Easter" derives from either a Teutonic goddess of spring (*Eastre* or *Eostre*), or from *Ostar*, "an Old Germanic root [word] for dawn or east (the time and place of the rising sun)," according to the *Evangelical Dictionary of Theology*. The most popular theory is that, at some point and for reasons now unknown, these two terms became synonymous with *Pascha*. Some scholars believe the word "Easter" replaced *Pascha* as a result of the pagan celebrations surrounding *Eostre,* while others are more inclined to see "Easter" as a reference to *Ostar* (the sun) and dawning of the spring (which would be consistent as a symbol of Christ).

The truth probably lies somewhere in the middle. Christians likely started making reference to their *Pascha* as "Easter" soon after 325 AD, when the Council of Nicea set its observance day. The timing happened to coincide loosely with the pagan festival celebrating the return of spring (April) and its goddess (*Eostre*).

The pagans feasted, held sunrise ceremonies, and observed special rituals to give thanks for the renewal and rebirth of life after the winter. Moreover, using "Ostar" for that portion of the year would certainly have been apropos, given the sun's increasing brightness.

So Christians of that era, it seems, saw an excellent opportunity to reach out to their non-Christian neighbors by linking *Pascha* to the pagan celebrations of renewal and rebirth. They, of course, put a Christian twist on it by pointing out that only through Christ and his resurrection could anyone experience *true* renewal and rebirth.

When the pagans saw Christians celebrating near the time of their own festivals, they probably just referred to what the Christians were doing as *Ostar/Eostre*. Soon, *Pascha* was being called the *Ostar/Eastre* festival more and more, until the name *Pascha* completely faded away.

The Roman Catholic monk and historian, Bede (c. 673–735), apparently witnessed this transition, explaining in his work *On the Reckoning of Time* about the month of April: "Eosturmonath [Easter month] has a name which is now translated 'Paschal month,' and which was once called after a goddess of theirs named Eostre, in whose honor feasts were celebrated in that month. Now they designate that Paschal season by her name, calling the joys of the new rite by the time honored name of the old observance."

Over time, Christians went even further by slowly adopting Pagan *Ostar/Eastre* symbols and infusing them with meanings to point unbelievers to Christ, the risen Lord. Most of the symbols related to the Germanic goddess of spring, pagan views of life, and fertility rites. Those symbols continue to be fascinating in their own ways and can still be used today as witnessing tools to discuss Christ with secular observers of Easter.

Here we see the beauty of symbols—they can be adapted and adopted to represent different things to different people. This was particularly advantageous during the years when Christianity began flourishing across the Roman Empire. Colored eggs, gift baskets, the Easter Bunny, parades, wearing one's best or new clothes, all of these aspects of Easter derive from paganism, specifically its folklore and mythology.

As troubling as this may sound to some Christians, use of such symbols need not cause too much concern since the church often has taken pagan symbols and adapted them to Christian use.

A World of Difference

Many Languages, One Message

For all of you who were baptized into Christ have clothed yourselves with Christ. There is neither Jew nor Greek, slave nor free, male nor female, for you are all one in Christ Jesus.

Galatians 3:27–28 NIV

In any language—*Paasfeest, Ostern, Pasqua, Uskrs, Paskalya*—Easter basically means the same thing: Christ is risen!

To express this magnificent belief, Christians observe different traditions based on their ethnic backgrounds and cultural history. Some communities stress the joy of Easter stemming from Jesus' resurrection, while others concentrate more on the sorrow of the season, keeping Christ's sacrifice on the cross in the forefront.

Picturing the resurrection through a show of both jubilation and solemnity comes in many forms: concerts, special dances, church services, specific foods, and sacred rituals. Although each vibrant Easter symbol, custom, and image might be meaningful to the cultures that use them, each one ultimately does one thing—tells the world of our deliverance from the bondage of sin and the curse of death. As Jesus said to Martha, "'I am the resurrection and the life. He who believes in me will live, even if he dies'" (John 11:25 NIV).

Easter traditions, simply put, are the visible expressions of what the New Testament describes as the mission of all Christians—"to call people from among all the Gentiles to obedience that comes through faith" (Romans 1:5 NIV). Easter, therefore, is not only a worldwide celebration, it is an international season of evangelism. It is, especially for children, also a great time of fun.

Heavenly Signs

Do the Stars Foretell God's Plan?

God set them in the expanse of the sky to give light on the earth, to govern the day and the night, and to separate light from darkness. And God saw that it was good.

Genesis 1:17–18 NIV

Nature, according to Scripture, is not just some random by-product of chance, odds, survival of the fittest, or as secular scientists might call it, punctuated equilibria. It is the deliberate handiwork of God who "created the heavens and the earth" and pronounced it "good" (Genesis 1:1–4 NIV).

So it should come as no surprise that nature itself might provide symbols of the divine plan for salvation from sin through the death and resurrection of Christ. Some

Christians believe that God did indeed place signs within creation itself that, when interpreted in the light of ancient traditions and beliefs, present the gospel story through symbolic language.

The most popular (and controversial) theory on this is known as the "Gospel in the Stars," which holds that the Lord placed a message relating to the gospel story within each of the constellations in the ancient Zodiac. This idea was first popularized in *The Gospel in the Stars* by Joseph Seiss and *The Witness of the Stars* (1893) by E. W. Bullinger.

According to Seiss, "[A]ll the great doctrines of the Christian faith were known, believed, cherished, and recorded [in the stars] from the earliest generations of our race, proving that God has spoken to man, and verily given him a revelation of truths and hopes precisely as written in our Scriptures, and so fondly cherished by all Christian believers."

Bullinger, an Anglican minister, explained in detail his Christian interpretations of the Zodiac, claiming that pagans had corrupted the original godly meanings to ancient peoples:

Zodiac Constellation	**Traditional Image**	**Christian Interpretation**
Aries	Ram	Sacrifice
Taurus	Bull	Resurrection
Gemini	Twins	Christ's Dual Nature (God-Man)
Cancer	Crab	Redeemed Gathered Together
Leo	Lion	Christ the King
Virgo	Virgin	The Virgin Mary
Libra	Scales	Need for Sins Punished
Scorpio	Scorpion	Death Through Sin
Sagittarius	Archer	Demons
Capricorn	Goat	Corruption
Aquarius	Water-Pourer	Living Water/ Noah's Flood
Pisces	Fish	God's People

Whether the gospel story shines so clearly in the stars remains a topic of serious debate. Either way, it cannot be denied that Scripture says the "heavens declare the glory of God" (Psalms 19:1–4 NIV). Romans 1:19–20 also says we can discern certain aspects of God's character by observing creation (NIV).

At the very least, nature offers many useful symbols for representing key truths surrounding the Christian faith and even God himself. This holds especially true at Easter, the celebration of Jesus' resurrection.

All Creatures Great and Small

Lambs, Butterflies, and Birds

Nature is a revelation of God.

Henry Wadsworth Longfellow
1807–1882
American poet

The animal kingdom offers some of the most common, yet striking Easter symbols for Christ, his death, and resurrection. Some of them, like the lamb and butterfly, are fairly well known. Others, however, are not so familiar, but serve just as well to represent the Easter message.

Most common is the lamb, which often serves as a representation of Christ in scripture. This is due primarily to classic Jewish imagery that associated the lamb with sacrifice. The Old Testament, for example, refers to the Messiah, specifically as one who would be sacrificed as a lamb led to the slaughter. Isaiah 53:7 reads: "He was oppressed and afflicted, yet he did not open his mouth; he was led like a lamb to the slaughter, and as a sheep before her shearers is silent, so he did not open his mouth" (NIV).

And in the New Testament, Jesus is plainly referred to as "the Lamb of God" (John 1:29), the Passover/Paschal Lamb (1 Corinthians 5:7), and the lamb who was slain "without defect or blemish" (1 Peter 1:19 NIV).

To highlight this imagery, many churches erect pictures of a lamb for viewing for the seven days prior to Easter morning (Holy Week). If the lamb is lying down, it represents the Lord on whom our iniquities were placed, "We, all like sheep, have gone astray, each of us has turned to his own way; and the Lord has laid on him the iniquity of us all" (Isaiah 53:6 NIV). If the lamb is standing, it points more toward the triumphant Christ as the resurrected Lamb of God.

In *Our Christian Symbols*, Friedrich Rest explains, "Sometimes the lamb carries a resurrection banner, or a white pennant with a red cross." He adds: "The white pennant represents the body of Christ, which is attached to the cruciform staff, representing the cross on which the Lamb of God died and through which the risen Christ saves the world."

As for the butterfly, it is not actually mentioned in Scripture. Nevertheless, it has come to represent the Easter miracle because it emerges as a beautiful creature (resurrection) after being "entombed" in a cocoon (death). Like the lamb, the butterfly adorns many church banners as a symbol of not only Christ, but also of individual believers and the resurrection they are to receive.

Interestingly, the ancient Greek word for the butterfly was *psyche,* which additionally meant the soul or breath of life. It was so named by the Greek philosopher Aristotle (384 BC–322 BC). Even before him, the ancient Egyptians were connecting the creature with one's soul, believing that the butterfly would be one of the many visual pleasures enjoyed by the deceased in the afterlife.

Christians in the first and second centuries probably adopted the butterfly as a symbol for the resurrection because the Romans and Greeks drew the soul in the form of a butterfly. The butterfly is also a symbol of the soul in Roman, Aztec, Mexican (especially in the towns of Rosario and Angangueo), Russian, Spanish, German, and Irish (c. 1600s) cultures.

Another animal that remains a symbol of the resurrection, although not as popular as it used to be, is the rooster. It "first appeared on weather vanes, cathedral towers, and domes during the Middle Ages," writes Martha R. Fehl and Randy Bishop in "Where'd the Eggs and Bunnies Come From?" *Today's Christian,* March/April 1998 (www.christianitytoday.com). The main inspiration for making the rooster a symbol of Easter can be found in Matthew 26, where Peter denies Christ three times—just as Jesus had predicted during the Last Supper (NIV).

"Then he began to call down curses on himself and he swore to them, 'I don't know the man!' Immediately a rooster crowed. Then Peter remembered the words Jesus had spoken: 'Before the rooster crows, you will disown me three times.' And he went outside and wept bitterly" (Matthew 26:74–75 NIV).

Finally, it would be remiss not to mention baby chicks, represented every year not only by PEEPS® (marshmallow candies in yellow, purple, and pink), but also by live chicks given as gifts. Baby chicks—all baby animals, for that matter—symbolize the resurrection to many Christians because they represent new life. Little chicks, however, have a special link to Easter as the ones that burst forth from an egg, just as Christ burst forth from the tomb.

Week Five

Signs and Wonders

The Flora of Easter

Parables in Bloom

Consider how the lilies grow. They do not labor or spin. Yet I tell you, not even Solomon in all his splendor was dressed like one of these.

Luke 12:27 NIV

No one knows precisely when the lily became an Easter tradition, but it may descend from a legend about lilies found in the Garden of Gethsemane after Jesus' death and resurrection. Exquisite lilies, so the story goes, miraculously sprang to life where Christ's drops of sweat/blood fell while praying in the garden on the night he was betrayed. "And being in anguish, he prayed more earnestly, and his sweat was like drops of blood falling to the ground" (Luke 22:44 NIV).

In addition to being a symbol of Christ's resurrection, the lily often represents the Virgin Mary. This connection to Jesus' mother can be traced to an ancient link between the flower and motherhood.

This flower—called the "white apostle of hope"—has remained one of the most popular symbols for Jesus' resurrection, partly due to the Luke 12:27 reference (see above) to the bloom as having "splendor" comparable to that of Solomon's.

In Hosea 14:5–6, the lily is actually a picture of Israel. "I will be like the dew to Israel; he will blossom like a lily . . . his fragrance like a cedar of Lebanon (NIV). And in Song of Solomon 2:1–2, the lily stands for someone's beloved: "I am a rose of Sharon, a lily of the valleys. Like a lily among thorns is my darling among the maidens" (NIV).

Taken together, these three references easily paint a picture of Christ—the glorious beloved of Israel. Furthermore, its white color easily represents the Lord's purity, innocence, radiant life, vitality, and new beginnings.

It was almost predictable that plants and flowers would become Easter symbols. They have always been closely associated with spring, which is itself a symbol of resurrection, new life, and regeneration.

"It is a time of promise, of newness, of renewal of hope. The long dark nights and desolation of winter are passing," explained Jim Bishop of Eastern Mennonite University in an Easter article, "Symbol of Suffering and Death Offer New Life." Consequently, tulips, daffodils, and narcissus are also popular at Easter, primarily because they bloom in the spring. All flowers that "spring forth" are seen as signs of rejuvenation and of how new life can emerge out of death.

The pomegranate fruit, while not a flower, is yet another Easter emblem for two reasons: its many seeds represent an abundance of life; and its deep red color is suggestive of blood, a biblical symbol of life. "For the life of a creature is in the blood, and I have given it to you to make atonement for yourselves . . . because the life of every creature is its blood. . . ." (Leviticus 17:11–14 NIV).

Within Jewish culture, blood has long been a symbol for eternal life. So, the pomegranate, with its blood-red juice, fits perfectly with Christ's promise to grant eternal life to those who place their faith in him.

The Legend of the Dogwood

Blossoms Bearing Witness

They put a purple robe on him, then twisted together a crown of thorns and set it on him.

Mark 15:17 NIV

One plant, the dogwood, has become a popular Easter legend of its own. It has come to represent Jesus' death and resurrection because its four-petal shape brings to mind the cross, the markings on the petals resemble nail marks, and the center of the blooms recall Christ's crown of thorns.

Although the Bible does not mention the kind of wood the Romans used for Jesus' cross, a recurring story, in various forms, has consistently put the dogwood in that role. According to legend:

> At the time of Christ's death, the dogwood tree was as tall and solid as the mighty oak. Its wood was so strong, in fact, that the Roman soldiers in charge of executing Jesus decided to use the trunk of a nearby dogwood to fashion a cross for him. During his crucifixion, Christ sensed the tree's sorrow over being used in such a way, and the Lord felt compassion toward it. So he told the tree, "Because of your regret about what has befallen you, and because of your pity on me, you shall never again be used as an instrument of death. From this day forward, instead of growing thick, and tall, and straight, you shall grow slender, bent, and fragile, with a flower showing petals that form a cross, each of which

has a nail print mark on its outer edge. In the center of your bloom will be a crown of thorns, stained brown and rusty, so all who behold it will remember who died upon your branches. And your red berries will reflect the color of my blood shed for all humanity. This is my blessing to you, so you will never again be mutilated, destroyed, or made an object of shame. Instead, you will be cherished and protected as a symbol of my loving sacrifice."

A Sand Dollar's Tale

Rich Symbols in a Tiny Shell

And God said, "Let the water teem with living creatures, and let birds fly above the earth aross the expanse of the sky." So God created the great creatures of the sea and every living and moving thing with which the water teems, according to their kinds, and every winged bird to its kind. And God saw that it was good.

Genesis 1:20–21 NIV

The markings on the beautiful and intricate sand dollar have earned it a role in the Easter celebration. Similar to the way the dogwood became associated with Christianity, no one knows how or when the shell of this tiny sea creature started representing Christ's birth, death, and resurrection;

but many versions of the sand dollar legend circulate every Easter season. Each one appears in a poem that describes the various facets of the shell and often appears on greeting cards, plaques, and gift items. Like all symbols, the sand dollar serves as an imprint of sacred beliefs and a tool for sharing those beliefs with others.

Version One

(Seattle Post Intelligencer, 1966)

There's a pretty little legend, that I would like to tell,
Of the birth and death of Jesus, found in this
lowly shell.
If you examine closely, you'll see that you
find here,
Four nail holes and a fifth one, made by a
Roman's spear.
On one side the Easter lily, its center is the star,
That appeared unto the shepherds, and led them
from afar.

The Christmas poinsettia, etched on the other side,
Reminds us of His birthday, our happy
Christmastide.
Now break the center open, and here you will
release,
The five white doves awaiting, to spread good will
and peace.
This simple little symbol, Christ left for you and me,
To help us spread His Gospel, through all eternity.

Version Two

(anonymous/unknown)

Upon this odd-shaped sea shell, a legend grand
is told,
About the life of Jesus, the wondrous tale of old.
The center marking plainly shows, the well known
Guiding Star,
That led to tiny Bethlehem, the wise men from
afar.
The Christmas flower, poinsettia, for his
Nativity,

The resurrection, too, is marked, the Easter
Lily see.
Five wounds were suffered by our Lord, from nails
and Roman's spear,
When He died for us on the cross, the wounds
show plainly here.
Within the shell, should it be broke, five doves of
peace are found,
To emphasize this legend, so may Love and Peace
abound.

Version Three

by Richard Abanes

Behold God's wondrous creation, the sand dollar
of old,
Divinely etched upon its shell, a story to be told.
The lily in the center, looking like a star,
Reflects the guiding light that led, the wise men
from afar.
And around the star, four tiny marks, as if it were
impaled,

Reminders of Christ's wounds for us, when his
hands and feet were nailed,
Another cut upon the shell, brings the memory
near,
Of Christ, whose side was pierced so deep, by a
Roman spear.
Now on the other side, a poinsettia you will see,
Hearkens back with joyful thanks, to the Nativity.
Now open up this tiny shell, and five doves will
be found,
The love and peace, the hope and joy, and faith
that now abound.

The Mythical Phoenix

Ancient Symbol of Rebirth

Even by a bird He shows us the mightiness of His power.

Clement of Rome
AD 30–100
An early bishop

Undoubtedly, the Phoenix is the most famous pagan symbol that was given an Easter meaning. By ancient accounts, this mythical bird of unmatched splendor and extraordinarily long life (about 500 years) was the size of a large eagle with red and gold plumage around its neck, a purple body, and an azure tail.

A legend that began in Egypt, several thousand years before Christ, holds that when the bird had reached the end of its life, it would build a special nest (a funeral pyre) made of myrrh and aromatic branches. Then, on its last night of life, the Phoenix would sit in the nest and await the sunrise. At dawn, beneath the sun's rays, the nest would burst into flames and consume the Phoenix. Out of the ashes would rise a new Phoenix, young and strong, reborn to live another five centuries.

For thousands of years this legend spread throughout the world until the Phoenix represented regeneration, immortality, and rebirth for not only the Egyptians, but also for the Greeks, Romans, Persians, and other ancient peoples. For obvious reasons, the bird quickly came to represent Christ, beginning with Clement of Rome (AD 30–100), who was the first Christian to connect the Phoenix to Jesus and the resurrection.

Clement even titled his text, "The Phoenix An Emblem of Our Resurrection," asking: "Do we then deem it any great and wonderful thing for the Maker of all things to raise up again those that have piously served Him in the assurance of a good faith, when even by a bird He shows us the mightiness of His power to fulfill His promise?"

Tertullian (c. 160/170–c. 215/220), an early Christian writer, also mentioned the Phoenix in his writings:

> The Phoenix Is Made A Symbol of Our Resurrection Bodies. . . . I refer to the bird which is peculiar to the East, famous for its singularity, marvellous from its posthumous life, which renews its life in a voluntary death; its dying day is its birthday, for on it, it departs and returns; once more a phoenix where just now there was none, once more himself, but just now out of existence; another, yet the same.

The parallels between the Phoenix and Jesus' resurrection are brought out every Easter as a symbol of a voluntary death, rising to new life, and immortality. "The reason my Father loves me is that I lay down my life—only to take it up again. No one takes it from me, but I lay it down of my own accord. I have authority to lay it down and authority to take it up again. This command I received from my Father" (John 10:17–18 NIV).

The Phoenix, understandably, appears in Christian art all over the world; as far back as the first few centuries of the church, including etchings in the walls of Rome's catacombs.

Believing in the Easter Bunny

Embodiment of Life and Sacrifice

"Cottontail, Peter Cottontail! How much better sounding that is than Peter Rabbit! That sounds as if I really was somebody. Yes, Sir, that's the very name I want. Now I must send word to all my friends that hereafter I am no longer Peter Rabbit, but Peter Cottontail."

Thornton W. Burgess
1874–1965
Author *The Adventures of Peter Cottontail*

Like most of the secular Easter symbols, the rabbit (or more accurately, the hare) originated in antiquity with the goddess Eostre. The cute little creature according to European mythology, was her favorite woodland creature. It was, therefore, sacred—a venerated symbol of spring.

The hare's hyper-fertility is another reason for its adoption long ago as a symbol of life and eventually as an Easter symbol. For instance, while still pregnant with one litter, a female hare can conceive a second litter! Moreover, hares/rabbits are able to bear young at an extraordinarily early age, and once they start producing offspring, can give birth to several litters a year. In the ancient world, pagans celebrated this fertility in spring at the time of the Eostre festival, which eventually became associated with the Christian celebration of resurrection, Easter.

In Germany, a folklore character known as *Oschter Haws* supposedly laid multi-colored eggs in nests the night before Easter morning. Immigrants from Deutschland, who settled in Pennsylvania, later introduced this figure in America, giving rise to the Easter Bunny. According to Ruth M. Reichmann of the Max Kade German-American Center (Indiana University-Perdue University, Indianapolis), this story about the Oschter Haws dates as far back as 1682.

German immigrants are also credited with introducing the custom of having children make nests for the rabbits, using hats or fancy paper boxes, says Susan E. Richardson in *Holidays & Holy Days*. Then, at some point in time, children began to be told that the furry, floppy-eared creature was the dispenser of Easter baskets filled with candy, gifts and colored eggs; similar to the way Santa Claus brings gifts and the Tooth Fairy brings coins.

Both the Easter Bunny and colored eggs, although extremely secular, can be given (and indeed, have been given) Christian meanings in many different churches. Consider the interpretation of the Easter Bunny by Nick Brown of the Orthodox Research Institute:

> [F]or the ancient Romans, the rabbit also had another meaning—that of sacrifice and salvation. The Romans believed that if a predator threatened a warren of rabbits, one solitary rabbit would surface from the burrow to offer itself as a sacrifice to appease the predator in an act that would save the other rabbits within the warren. Hence, when this symbol is viewed in the light of Christianity and Christ's resurrection, we are reminded that death was the predator that preyed on humanity, and that Christ through his own death on the cross was able to not only save us, but he was also able to kill death itself.

The hare and the egg came together at some point in history to jointly symbolize what they each stood for individually: life, spring, fertility, rebirth, and plenty. Those themes fit perfectly with Easter. "We were therefore buried with him through baptism into death in order that, just as Christ was raised from the dead through the glory of the Father, we too may live a new life" (Romans 6:4 NIV).

The Incredible, Edible Symbol

Colored Eggs Have Ancient Meanings

Indeed, He is risen!

Russian greeting

The connection between colored eggs and Easter stretches back to the use of eggs in religious ceremonies and festivals near the beginning of history itself. The ancient Egyptians, for example, buried eggs in their tombs. The Romans and Greeks saw eggs as symbols of life, rebirth, and/or abundance. An old Latin proverb sums up this perennial view: "All life comes from an egg." It is only natural that eggs were readily associated with Easter.

Interestingly, long before there even was an Easter, eggs were already being painted with bright colors, given away as gifts, and eaten at festivals celebrating the return of spring. Those wealthy enough to afford the extravagance often covered the eggs in gold leaf. The poor simply dyed the eggs by boiling them with assorted leaves and/or flower petals to yield different colors.

By the turn of the nineteenth century, the Pennsylvania Germans or Deutsch in the United States (eventually nicknamed Pennsylvania "Dutch") were holding yearly celebrations that featured games, egg hunts, and eating contests. Egg hunts eventually became popular throughout America.

Eggs have long been popular and meaningful within the Christian tradition, too. "The concept of eggs as life went hand in hand with the concept of eggs as emblems of immortality," Tamra Andrews notes in *Nectar and Ambrosia: An Encyclopedia of Food in World Mythology.* "Easter eggs, in fact, symbolize immortality, and particularly the resurrection of Christ, who rose from a sealed tomb just as a bird breaks through an eggshell."

This is why in some churches, Easter eggs are called Pace Eggs, the word "Pace" being a derivative of *Pesah* (Passover). As far back as the fourth century, pagans who converted to Christianity felt that the egg was a perfect symbol for Christ, the source and giver of life. As Christians, they continued giving eggs as gifts, just as they had done before their conversion, but after accepting Jesus as their savior, they used them as expressions of the eternal life and rebirth available in Christ.

The famous Ukrainian pysanky eggs, once used as pagan amulets to ward off evil spirits, underwent a radical transformation in meaning after Christianity was introduced to the Ukraine in 988 AD. They came to symbolize Jesus' triumph over death through his resurrection and the rising of the Son of God from the darkened depths of the grave.

Many churches in the East still use eggs in this manner at their Easter meals. As Nick Brown, writes in "Pascha: Festivities and Symbols," www.orthodoxresearchinstitute.org:

> The red colouring [of the shell] stands for the blood that was shed for us on the cross. The outer casing on the shell represents the tomb that Christ was interred into. . . . When we crack the eggs with each other to reveal the insides, we are in effect recreating the effect of Christ rising from the tomb, just as a newborn chick is released from the confines of the eggshell when it receives new life. This is the other important meaning; new Life.

Other customs surrounding Pace Eggs abound. In Yugoslavia, Russia, and the Ukraine, the initials "XB" (representing the Cyrillic letters for *Khrystos Voskres*) are inscribed on Easter eggs and stands for "Christ is risen." This is also the greeting/ blessing used in Russia when Christians exchange red-dyed eggs on Easter. The response is *Voistinu Voskrese* ("Indeed, He is risen!")

The British celebration of Easter Sunday includes comical races where participants roll hard-boiled eggs down hills. The winner is the one whose egg rolls the farthest or lasts the longest before breaking. In the United States, the White House traditionally hosts an Easter Egg Roll for children each year on the Monday after Easter. According to the official White House Web site, it was recorded in the press as early as 1872.

Another English tradition is "jarping," a game that has players cracking their hard-boiled eggs against the eggs of others. The last one with an unbroken egg, having shown fortitude and perseverance in the face of many competitors (sometimes a game of jarping can take all day), wins. For Christians, such fortitude represents a person's perseverance in Christ and the winner is declared blessed of God.

Clearly, Christians can use colored eggs, like other secular symbols of the holiday, as great illustrations for what Christ accomplished through his death and resurrection. The eggs might have been overtly pagan, but have taken on new meanings that faithful followers of Jesus Christ can enjoy.

The Colors of Faith

Many Shades of Meaning

We are symbols and inhabit symbols.

Ralph Waldo Emerson
1803–1882
Essayist and poet

People of various cultures have used colors for thousands of years to represent personality traits, emotions, and human concepts (for example, good and evil). It is no surprise, then, that Christians would have used them to help remember aspects of their faith.

Three colors—all of which have their meanings taken from Scripture—are important at Easter: white, black, and violet/purple. These colors gained their biblical symbolism by repeated use throughout ancient cultures. The *Dictionary of Biblical Imagery* tells us, "[They] are symbolic because of their primary association with elements of nature and their use within the cultures of the biblical times."

White is usually set in opposition to black throughout Scripture as the color of God's redemption and acceptance (light) in contrast to his judgment and wrath (darkness). Consider the white garments worn by the faithful saints pictured in the Book of Revelation. They show that the redeemed are pure and acceptable to God: "Then each of them was given a white robe" (Revelation 6:11 NIV). Believers are likewise described by Isaiah as having their sins washed white as snow. "Though your sins are like scarlet, they shall be as white as snow" (Isaiah 1:18 NIV). And Christ himself—the Ancient of Days—is said to be dressed in white. "His clothing was as white as snow; the hair of his head was white like wool" (Daniel 7:9 NIV).

However, when God is shown descending to the earth in anger, he is wrapped in darkness. "He parted the heavens and came down; dark clouds were under his feet. . . . He made darkness his covering" (Psalms 18:9–11 NIV). Similarly, the Lord's day of judgment itself is called "a day of darkness and gloom, a day of clouds and blackness" (Joel 2:2 NIV). And when Christ died on the cross, thereby paying the penalty of sin and satisfying God's judgment against unrighteousness, "darkness came over all the land" (Matthew 27:45 NIV).

Purple/violet in Scripture always suggests royalty, power, and/or wealth. This is because during biblical times the dye needed to make the color was very expensive. Only nobility could afford purple/violet clothes: "The king called out for the enchanters, astrologers and diviners to be brought and said to these wise men of Babylon, 'Whoever reads this writing and tells me what it means will be clothed in purple and have a gold chain placed around his neck, and he will be made the third highest ruler in the kingdom'" (Daniel 5:7 NIV).

Sadly, the familiar symbolism was used to mock Jesus when the soldiers who crucified him placed a purple/violet robe over his shoulders. "The soldiers twisted together a crown of thorns and put it on his head. They clothed him in a purple robe" (John 19:2 NIV).

After this incident, elements of mourning, humility, and suffering were imparted to the color. Such attributes are actually quite appropriate when viewed in light of God's mandate in the Old Testament to drape the bronze altar of the tabernacle (the altar on which the sacrificial animals were burned) with a purple/violet cloth whenever it was moved. "They are to remove the ashes from the bronze altar and spread a purple cloth over it" (Numbers 4:13 NIV).

During Easter, each of these colors show up on banners, in floral decorations, and for candles. They also appear in the vestments worn by Roman Catholic priests and Protestant ministers (for example, Presbyterian and Anglican): Lenten Sundays—Violet; Lenten weekdays and Saturdays, until Good Friday—Violet; Good Friday—Black; Easter and subsequent Sundays—White.

Some parents have cleverly and creatively blended the use of colors at Easter with the tradition of giving jelly beans. By doing so they teach their young children Christian beliefs. Each jelly bean color symbolizes a different aspect either of Christ's character or of the Easter story, as the following children's poem by an unknown author outlines:

Black is for the sins we made,
Red is for the price he paid,

Green is for the grass outside his grave,
White is for the grace to us he freely gave,
Orange is for the edge of night,
Yellow is for the sun so bright,
Purple is for his hour of sorrow,
Pink is for our new tomorrow. . . .

Week Six

A Time For Traditions

Hot Cross Buns

Pastry with a Past

Hot cross buns,
Hot cross buns,
one ha'penny,
two a penny,
hot cross buns.

Traditional lyrics attributed to
English street hawkers

The Irish, the English and Australians serve hot cross buns—the most common Easter food. Bakers decorate these treats, generally made with leavening, spices and currants, with a cross on top. They date at least to the early 1700s. The 1733 edition of *Poor Robin's Almanack* said: "Good Friday comes this month, the old woman runs, with one or two a penny hot cross buns." Another reference is in James Boswell's *Life of Johnson* (1791): "Being Good Friday I breakfasted with him and cross-buns."

Egyptian, Roman, and Greek pagans used to bring similar pastries to their temples as offerings before the advent of Christianity. The buns were ceremoniously marked with an ox drawing to represent the animal they normally sacrificed to the gods. Such rituals faded into obscurity when Christians replaced the ox with a cross to represent Christ, and used it as a food to celebrate the Lord's resurrection.

Because the buns were closely associated with the Roman Catholic Church, the buns fell out of favor in Britain after the Anglican split from the church in the 16th century. But efforts to entirely ban them failed because of their popularity. So Queen Elizabeth I reportedly decreed that bakers could sell them—but only for Easter, Christmas, and funerals. They especially remained a Good Friday favorite.

"I am the bread of life. Your forefathers ate the manna in the desert, yet they died. But here is the bread that comes down from heaven, which a man may eat and not die. I am the living bread that came down from heaven. If anyone eats of this bread, he will live forever. The bread is my flesh, which I will give for the life of the world" (John 6:48–51 NIV).

Blessing of the Baskets

Praising God's Abundance

Give, and it will be given to you. A good measure, pressed down, shaken together and running over, will be poured into your lap. For with the measure you use, it will be measured to you.

Luke 6:38 NIV

The tradition of giving Easter baskets to friends and family is an offshoot of the ancient ritual observed by farmers who would bring their first crops and seedlings to a nearby temple in hopes that this offering would insure a bountiful harvest. Roman Catholics later adopted the tradition, taking food intended for Easter to the church to be blessed. That practice was in turn mixed with Pennsylvania Dutch stories about *Oschter*

Haws (the Easter hare or rabbit) and his nest of brightly colored eggs. The result is today's popular Easter basket filled with sweet and savory treats.

In this mix was another tradition observed by German families of the eighteenth century—parents would have children place their straw-filled caps and bonnets out doors. In the morning, they would be filled with candy and hard-boiled eggs.

Eventually baskets replaced the caps and bonnets and grew larger to include a wide variety of foods serving as Christian symbols. Families also began placing a decorated candle next to the other articles and draping the entire Easter basket with a linen cover embroidered with a symbol for Jesus and the words "Christ is Risen."

An excellent visual explanation of the Easter basket and how to arrange one comes from the article "How to Put Together a Traditional

Easter Basket" by the Reverend Basil Kraynyak of the Greek Catholic Union (http://www.carpatho-rusyn.org/customs/easter.htm):

Easter Bread (Paska): "Symbolic of Christ Himself who is our True Bread. . . . Sometimes a cross of dough is placed on top encircled by a plait giving it a crowned effect, or Greek abbreviations for the name of Christ."

Cheese: "A custard-type cheese . . . having a rather bland but sweet taste indicative of the moderation that Christians should have in all things."

Ham: "[T]he main dish because of its richness and symbolic of the great joy and abundance of Easter."

Butter: "This favorite dairy product is shaped into the figure of a lamb or small cross and decorated as the cheese [is decorated]."

Sausage: "[I]ndicative of God's favor and generosity."

Bacon: "Symbolic of the overabundance of God's mercy to us."

Eggs: "Indicative of new life and resurrection."

Salt: "A condiment necessary for flavor, reminding the Christian of his duty to others."

Horseradish: "Symbolic of the Passion of Christ still in our minds but sweetened with some sugar because of the Resurrection. A bitter-sweet red colored mixture reminds us of the sufferings of Christ."

Preparing such a basket for Easter is extremely important in Eastern churches and stands as a prime example of a secular tradition Christianized. For Polish-Americans, *Swieconka* ("Blessing of the Baskets") is an essential part of Easter. The baskets and the foods inside are blessed with a specific prayer (a ceremony called *Poswiecenie Pokarmow*).

The Blessing of the Breads focuses on Jesus as the bread of life who died and rose again. The Blessing of the Meats relates to Christ as the Passover Lamb of God who takes away the sins of the world, and the Blessing of the Eggs points to Jesus as the source of new life.

Hosanna! Hosanna!
Enter the King!

"The next day the great crowd that had come for the Feast heard that Jesus was on his way to Jerusalem. They took palm branches and went out to meet him, shouting, 'Hosanna! Blessed is he who comes in the name of the Lord! Blessed is the King of Israel!' Jesus found a young donkey and sat upon it, as it is written, 'Do not be afraid, O Daughter of Zion; see, your king is coming, seated on a donkey's colt.'"

John 12:12–15 NIV

Palm Sunday marks the triumphant entrance of Jesus into Jerusalem and the beginning of Holy Week, the last days leading up to Christ's crucifixion. It is traditionally a day of sorrow as well as rejoicing—sorrow because the day is indicative of the nearness of Christ's death; joy because it heralds his imminent triumph over death as the King of Kings.

Also noteworthy about Palm Sunday is how Jesus' act of coming into Jerusalem on a colt that no one had "ever ridden" (Luke 19:30) was a fulfillment of the Messianic prophecy found in Zechariah 9:9: "Shout, Daughter of Jerusalem! See, your king comes to you, righteous and having salvation, gentle and riding on a donkey, on a colt, the foal of a donkey" (NIV).

It is not surprising that "the crowd that went ahead of him and those that followed shouted, 'Hosanna [save us] to the Son of David'" (Matthew 21:9 NIV). Luke 19:38 further reveals that the people cried out, "Blessed is the king who comes in the name of the Lord." And John 12:13 adds that those present boldly announced, blessed is "the king of Israel!"

This event appears to be a direct parallel to Psalm 118:25–26: "O LORD, save us, O LORD grant us success. Blessed is he who comes in the name of the LORD. From the house of the LORD we bless you."

Psalms 118, interestingly, is the very same one that the Jews would sing as they approached Jerusalem for Passover. They also used it to conclude the Passover meal. This has led some biblical commentators to interpret their shouts of adulation as a kind of foreshadow of Christ's death as their sacrificial lamb (because he died at Passover). At the very least, it signified their recognition of him as Messiah.

The day is called *Palm* Sunday because the people welcomed Christ by laying large palm branches on the road before him, a common custom in the Middle East, signifying that a person was worthy of great honor. For this reason, many Christian churches distribute palms to worshipers on Palm Sunday.

The palm frond in the Jewish tradition of Christ's day stood for victory and triumph as seen in the Feast of Tabernacles. "On the first day you are to take choice fruit from the trees, and palm fronds, leafy branches and poplars and rejoice before the Lord your God for seven days" (Leviticus 23:40 NIV).

Using similar imagery, part of John's apocalyptic vision reads "before me was a great multitude that no one could count . . . They were wearing white robes and were holding palm branches in their hands" (Revelation 7:9 NIV).

Today, the significance of the palm has developed into many different customs. Throughout Finland, for example, the people take willow twigs on Palm Sunday and lightly tap each other with them on the legs or back. This signifies one's wishes for them to have a blessed and fruitful year. In return, the one whisked by the willow gives the person who tapped them a small gift on Easter, for example, a coin, some candy, or an egg.

In Huaraz, Peru, Christians place an effigy of Jesus on a donkey and carry it into the city on Palm Sunday as a reenactment of Christ's entrance into Jerusalem. In Mexico, Holy Week begins with the "Blessing of the Palms." Churches later burn these palms and use the ashes the following year to draw a cross on the foreheads of Ash Wednesday churchgoers.

Where Jesus Walked

Gathering in the Holy Land

I tell you, I will not drink of this fruit of the vine from now on until that day when I drink it anew with you in My Father's kingdom. And when they had sung a hymn, they went out to the Mount of Olives.

Matthew 26:29–30 NIV

The Holy Land, where the very first Easter occurred, is understandably a place of extremely fervent celebrations and rituals surrounding the death and resurrection of Jesus. Holy Week begins on Palm Sunday as thousands of Christians from all over the world gather at the Mount of Olives to reenact Jesus' entry into Jerusalem. As in so many other countries, they wave palm branches, stopping momentarily at the Dominus Flevit ("The Lord Wept") a tear-shaped church that supposedly marks the spot where Jesus wept over the city and prophesied his coming death.

"As he approached Jerusalem and saw the city, he wept over it and said, 'If you, even you, had only known on this day what would bring you peace—but now it is hidden from your eyes'" (Luke 19:41–42 NIV).

As the Holy Week progresses, countless believers flock to Jerusalem to visit such historic sites such as the Coenaculum, which is said to be the hall where Christ held the Last Supper with the disciples and the Garden of Gethsemane where Jesus prayed prior to his betrayal. "He will show you a large upper room, all furnished. Make preparations there" (Luke 22:12 NIV). "Then Jesus went with his disciples to a place called Gethsemane, and he said to them, 'Sit here while I go over there and pray'" (Matthew 26:36 NIV).

No Greater Love

The Master Serves

A new command I give you: Love one another. As I have loved you, so you must love one another.

John 13:34 NIV

The Thursday before Easter is called Maundy Thursday after the Latin word *mandatum*, from which we get the English word "mandate." It literally means a command, and in relation to this particular holy day, refers to Christ's command for us to "love one another" (John 13:34 NIV). As early as the fourth century, special services took place on the Mount of Olives and at Gethsemane to celebrate this day.

Two hundred years later, the widespread observance of this day included a Blessing of

Oils and a restoration to the church of those who were estranged from God. By the sixth century, foot washings had been added to Maundy Thursday in remembrance and imitation of Christ, who washed the feet of his disciples during his last meal with them.

"After that, he poured water into a basin and began to wash his disciples' feet, drying them with the towel that was wrapped around him. . . . 'Now that I, your Lord and Teacher, have washed your feet, you also should wash one another's feet'" (John 13: 5–14 NIV).

In many churches, such a practice is also connected (like so many other aspects of Lent) to baptism because of imagery invoked by using water.

Believers observe this holy day with great reverence, as well as some degree of sorrow, since it occurs on the day Jesus had his last meal with the disciples, after which he was betrayed, arrested, and placed on trial throughout the night.

In remembrance of these events, especially the Last Supper, communion is held during the Maundy Thursday church services—whether Protestant, Roman Catholic, or Eastern Orthodox. The most important facet of Maundy Thursday, however, is the example that Christ set when he washed the feet of his disciples.

The selfless act dramatically demonstrated both humility and servanthood. His humble service takes on an added measure of solemnity and relevance to Christians when considered in light of the words he spoke as he washed their feet (see John 13:34 NIV).

What's So Good About Friday?

A Time to Mourn

"When the centurion and those with him who were guarding Jesus saw the earthquake and all that had happened, they were terrified, and exclaimed, 'Surely he was the Son of God!'"

Matthew 27:54 NIV

Good Friday, of course, is the day we commemorate the crucifixion of Christ. It is also called Passion Friday or the Day of Preparation, more commonly referred to as "good" Friday because of the blessings that flowed from Christ's sacrifice. The day, however, remains a somber one. To celebrate, some denominations hold long services. The Anglican Church, for instance, offers one that lasts from noon to 3 p.m. (mirroring the hours that Jesus hung on the cross). Some churches hold services to recite special prayers. Still others hold services built around a sermon (or sermons) based on Christ's final words from the cross:

1. "Father, forgive them, for they do not know what they are doing" (Luke 23:34 NIV).
2. "[T]oday, you will be with me in paradise" (Luke 23:43 NIV).
3. "Dear woman, here is your son!" (John 19:26 NIV).
4. "My God, my God, why have you forsaken me?" (Mark 15:34 NIV).
5. "I am thirsty" (John 19:28 NIV).
6. "It is finished" (John 19:30 NIV).
7. "Father, into your hands I commit my spirit" (Luke 23:46 NIV).

The day was first marked as an occasion for special observance around the fourth century with an exaltation of Christ's death through the popular "Veneration of the Cross" ceremony (still practiced in the Roman Catholic Church) in which believers may kneel, touch or kiss a large cross in adoration of Christ's sacrifice as part of the Good Friday service.

Today, myriad other traditions are also associated with Good Friday. Communion, for instance, is offered in many churches, along with passion reenactments, and ceremonial processions (inside churches, as well as outside on the street).

Prayer vigils are also common. Members of the Eastern Orthodox Church, in fact, meet three times for prayer: before noon (Royal Hours); afternoon (Vespers); and at night (Matins). The church adds visual imagery to help the congregants experience the events of the day.

In the morning, a large cross is set near the front or center of the church, and on it is placed a painted image of Christ. In the afternoon, it is later taken down and carried to the altar, where it rests with a shroud near a small table decorated with flowers—a representation of Jesus' tomb. Finally, in the evening, congregants use the shroud in a procession. Afterward, it is returned to the small table (the "tomb") to await Easter morning.

Other churches keep the main sanctuary dimly lit, the candles out, and various parts of the sanctuary draped in dark cloths. Such symbolism highlights the mourning of the day. It is, as Archbishop Ambrose (c. 339–397) said, a "day of bitterness," as quoted in Chris Armstrong's "The Goodness of Good Friday" (*Christianity Today*, 4/18/2003, www.christianitytoday.com).

Similarly, says Armstrong, the Apostolic Constitutions church manual of the fourth century called Good Friday a "day of mourning."

One of the most stirring Good Friday ceremonies that some churches practice is the Tenebrae, or Service of Darkness, which dates to the Medieval era. It begins with all the candles in the church lit. Then, one by one, each candle is extinguished until the entire congregation is seated in darkness. This represents, in a very tangible way, the darkness that covered the earth when Jesus died. "At the sixth hour darkness came over the whole land until the ninth hour" (Mark 15:33 NIV).

A loud noise is subsequently made (for example, a book dropped, a door slammed, or a cymbal struck) to symbolize the earthquake at Christ's death. "At that moment the curtain of the temple was torn in two from top to bottom. The earth shook and the rocks split" (Matthew 27:51 NIV).

A New Fire

The Eve of Easter

May all who are buried with Christ in the death of baptism rise also with him to newness of life.

From the Roman Catholic baptismal rite

Baptism is commonly scheduled for Pascha/Easter Sunday. The worship music, Scripture readings, and sermons usually include, at some point, the symbolic images of water and light, which are reminiscent of baptism and its spiritual significance as a picture of the believer's future resurrection.

Many churches today use the Paschal Candle, known as far back as the fourth century. Its light symbolizes not only Christ's divinity, but also his triumph over darkness (or death/evil), and his identity as the light of the world. "I am the light of the world. Whoever follows me will never walk in darkness, but will have the light of life" (John 8:12 NIV).

The lighting of this candle originated as part of the celebration that took place on the night before Easter morning. This evening—known variously as Holy Saturday, Grand Saturday, Angelic Night, or the Easter Vigil—for many centuries remained an important time of reflection and preparation for Easter morning.

This vigil began with the "blessing of the new fire"—that is, the lighting of the Paschal Candle. According to Herbert Thurston's article on the "Paschal Candle" in *The Catholic Encyclopedia*, this light was a special "column of wax of exceptional size, usually fixed in a great candlestick specially destined for that purpose."

The candle served as a centerpiece for

the ceremony, which started with a long prayer/chant/hymn called the "Exultet" (still recited today). At this time, the candle was decorated with incense and lit. Then, from the candle, "all the other candles [or lamps] in the sanctuary are lit." This represented Jesus, "The true light that gives light to every man," reads John 1:9 (NIV).

Before the era of electricity, such a display was nothing short of breathtaking. Similar lightings would take place in the streets for all too see, as the second century Christian Eusebius (c. 265–c. 339) described in his writings:

> "[The emperor] transformed the night of the sacred vigil into the brilliancy of day, by lighting throughout the whole city pillars of wax, while burning lamps illuminated every part, so that this mystic vigil was rendered brighter than the brightest daylight."

The ceremony of baptism that occurred during the vigil was appropriately called *photismos*, which means "illumination." It is believed that this label was a direct reference to Hebrews 10:32, where the words "being illuminated," according to some interpretations, refer to being baptized. As given in the Douay-Rheims Bible, the Scripture says: "But call to mind the former days, wherein, being illuminated, you endured a great fight of afflictions."

During this ceremony, those that Christ had illuminated—that is, the baptismal candidates—would stand around Jesus, the one true source of illumination, represented by the Paschal Candle. They each held a smaller candle, meaning that their lesser light had come from him.

Within today's Roman Catholic Church, at the Easter Vigil, just before converts are baptized, a brief history of the significance of water is also presented. It explains "its gift in creation, the Great Flood, the Red Sea, the Jordan, the water and blood that flowed from the Savior's side (itself symbolizing Baptism and Eucharist, or humanity and divinity)."

The Paschal Candle is then submerged in water as the priest proclaims: "May all who are buried with Christ in the death of baptism rise also with him to newness of life."

Roman Catholics additionally include a blessing of water at the Vigil. The priest may then use consecrated water for baptisms and other blessings. Parishioners may take some of this "Easter Water" to spread throughout their homes as a symbol of God's prayer and protection over the family. The following prayer is simultaneously said in variant forms:

> "Whatever this water touches in our home, may it be cleansed and delivered

from harm. May this family enjoy the Spirit of God, goodness, and peace. May anything opposed to God and us be banished, so that we who call upon your Holy Name may be protected from all evil. In the name of the Father, Son, and Holy Spirit. Amen."

Holy Week

THE HUMAN DRAMA

An Altar in Our Homes

Family Worship for Holy Week

Go home to your family and tell them how much the Lord has done for you, and how he has had mercy on you.

Mark 5:19 NIV

Easter is an ideal time for observing family traditions. They can be fun for children, as well as instructive. Holy Week is often the best time to start a countdown of sorts to Easter Sunday. The tradition of building a kind of Easter altar to the Lord is popular in many households.

The daily gathering of the family and the progressive building of the altar, followed by a Scripture reading and singing, not only serves to bring a family closer together, but can also remind everyone of why Easter is celebrated.

Palm Sunday: Gather at a central spot in the home (for example, the dinner table or the fireplace) and place some palm fronds (or a few green branches from a nearby tree) as a focal point. Have each family member give an example of how he or she has been changed by Christ during the previous year. [Bible Reading—"After Jesus had said this, he went on ahead, going up to Jerusalem. As he approached Bethphage and Bethany at the hill called the Mount of Olives, he sent two of his disciples, saying to them, 'Go to the village ahead of you, and as you enter it, you will find a colt tied there, which no one has ever ridden. Untie it and bring it here'" (Luke 19:28–30 NIV).]

Monday: Add to the altar several different items tied together in a rubber band (for example, markers, pencils, spoons, scissors) to represent the different kinds of sins that clutter our lives and bind us so tightly that we cannot move freely in Christ. Each family member then shares how sins have negatively affected his or her own life and the lives of others. [Bible Reading—"Now the Passover and the Feast of Unleavened Bread were only two days away, and the chief priests and the teachers of the law were looking for some sly way to arrest Jesus and kill him" (Mark 14:1 NIV).]

Tuesday: Add to the altar a notebook, some parchment, or perhaps even a personal digital assistant as a symbol of the many sins that we commit daily. Then, have a moment of silence, while each family member, within his or her own heart, confesses to God any sins of which they have not yet repented. [Bible Reading—"If we claim to be without sin, we deceive ourselves and the truth is not in us" (1 John. 1:8 NIV) and "He is the atoning sacrifice for our sins, and not only for ours but also for the sins of the whole world" (1 John 2:2 NIV).]

Wednesday: Add a dollar bill (or any denomination of currency) to the altar and contemplate the worldly cravings that can pull us away from God; money, success, popularity, personal goals, to name but a few. Then, have family members tell the others what they have been fasting for Lent and why [Bible Reading—"They were delighted and agreed to give him money. He consented, and watched for an opportunity to hand Jesus over to them when no crowd was present" (Luke 22:5–6 NIV).]

Maundy Thursday: Add a loaf of bread and a glass of wine or grape juice to the objects on the altar in memory of the Last Supper that Jesus held with his disciples. Then have a special communion service, bearing in mind the coming sacrifice of Christ commemorated on the following day. Allow family members to share feelings about what Jesus was willing to do for them. [First Bible Reading—"Then he took the cup, gave thanks and offered it to them, saying 'Drink from it, all of you. This is my blood of the covenant, which is poured out for many for the forgiveness of sins'" (Matthew 26:17–35 NIV). Second Bible reading, which may be used to close this service, along with washing each other's feet just as Jesus washed the feet of his disciples. "After that, he poured water into a basin and began to wash his disciples' feet, drying them with the towel that was wrapped around him" (John 13:1–10 NIV).] If your family plans to do this, add a bowl of water and a cloth to the altar next to the bread and wine.

Good Friday: To commemorate the death of Christ, add a cross of some kind to the altar (perhaps one that has been handmade by the children out of twigs). Have each family member read a portion of the Scripture that details the crucifixion. [Bible Reading—"When he had finished praying, Jesus left with his disciples and crossed the Kidron Valley. On the other side there was an olive grove, and he and his disciples went into it" (John 18:1–19:42 NIV).]

Holy Saturday: For this day of waiting, have each family member write a favorite Bible chapter and verse on paper and add it to the altar. Each person in turn reads the passage from the Bible and explains why it is so meaningful. Compare this form of sharing to how the disciples must have felt while waiting for the Lord's resurrection. Perhaps they, too, were thinking back on their most treasured memories from his days of teaching. [Bible Reading—verses chosen by family members.]

Easter Sunday: Resurrection Day has come at last! In celebration, have each family member place a special gift for someone else in the family on the altar; a gift that they believe will help that person always recall Christ's gift of eternal life to them through his death and resurrection. [Bible Reading—". . . But these are written that you may believe that Jesus is the Christ, the Son of God, and that by believing you may have life in his name" (John 20:1–31 NIV).]

The Passion of the Christ

Drama as a Teaching Aid

Then Pilate took Jesus and had him flogged. The soldiers twisted together a crown of thorns and put it on his head. They clothed him in a purple robe and went up to him again and again, saying, "Hail, king of the Jews!" And they struck him in the face.

John 19:1–3 NIV

Holy week is further accented every year by the world-renowned Passion Plays of Germany, Austria and other central European countries. These extremely detailed and professional dramas that have their roots in the Middle Ages, are traditionally presented on Good Friday and tell the story of Christ's crucifixion and resurrection.

"Passion" refers to the trial, suffering, and crucifixion of Jesus Christ. According to the Online Etymology Dictionary (www.etymonline.com), the term stems from the Latin word for suffering. Contrary to what some people believe, these Passion Plays were never considered entertainment. They were used to teach the gospel to the illiterate.

Oberammergau, Germany, hosts the most famous Passion Play, which lasts six hours. Performed every ten years, it began in 1634 as a thanksgiving for surviving a great plague. (For a history of the play, see www.oberammergau.de.)

The same is true in Mexico and South America, where the most famous of these plays occur in Columbia, Venezuela, Ecuador, and Brazil. They usually open with the Last Supper, proceed through Christ's betrayal, his judgment before Pontius Pilate, the carrying of the cross, his crucifixion, then finally, the resurrection.

Actors often rehearse for as long as a year for the production. Much to the dismay of visitors from other countries, these plays are extremely graphic/realistic, and include real whippings of the actor playing Jesus—and in extreme cases, his actual crucifixion (by being either tied or nailed to a cross). Unlike the European Passion Plays presented on stage, those in the Americas generally take place in the streets, around various buildings, and in open fields.

In South America, in addition to these reenactments, the whole Semana Santa (Holy Week) offers fiestas with street bands, dancers, religious processions, noisemakers (maracas), decorated homes and beach parties. These are joyous celebrations not only of Easter, but also of spring.

Viva Cristo Rey!

Running for Jesus

When you walk, your steps will not be hampered; when you run, you will not stumble.

Proverbs 4:12 NIV

Chile has its own twist on the procession rituals, the *correr a Christo* ("run to Christ"). It derives from colonial times when Roman Catholic priests traveled to the houses of the elderly and infirmed to give them Holy Communion the Sunday after Easter. During those days there were many bandits who wanted to steal the priests' valuable silver chalices. Cowboys (huases) would guard priests on the route from house to house, and along the way, they would all be refreshed with food and drink.

This tradition continues in our modern era with a daylong celebration throughout various regions of Chile, especially in and around Santiago. The day begins with a Roman Catholic mass, followed by a procession as the parish priest rides in a decorated carriage as in the days of old.

Chilean cowboys are joined in modern times by children on bicycles, drivers wheeling carts or wagons, and people running beside the carriage. Thousands turn out to view the parade, which stops periodically so the priest can visit select homes. The procession begins with the shout *Viva Cristo Rey!* ("Long Live Christ the King!")

[Note: the following source gives the date for this run to Jesus as the Sunday after Easter http://gosouthamerica.about.com/od/culfiestas/a/SemSantaChile.htm].

To Bear His Burdens

Stations of the Cross

There are those who still find the cross a stumbling block, and others consider it foolishness, but I am more convinced than ever before that it is the power of God unto social and individual salvation. So like the Apostle Paul I can now humbly say, I bear in my body the marks of the Lord Jesus. The suffering and agonizing moments through which I have passed over the last few years have also drawn me closer to God. More than ever I am convinced of the reality of a personal God.

The Rev. Dr. Martin Luther King Jr.
1929–1968
"Suffering and Faith," *Christian Century,* 1960

Jerusalem hosts the most widely known Good Friday procession in all of Christendom: the march along the fourteen Stations of the Cross leading to Golgotha. "They came to a place called Golgotha—which means The Place of a Skull" (Matthew 27:33 NIV). (Mark 15:22 and John 19:17 say virtually the same thing.)

This is the hill on which Christ died. "After they had mocked Him, they took off the robe and put his own clothes on Him. Then they led him away to crucify him. As they were going out, they met a man from Cyrene, named Simon, and they forced him to carry the cross" (Matthew 27:31–32 NIV).

The Via Dolorosa route—or the "Way of Suffering"—begins just inside the Old City, along the Ecce Homo archway near the Lion's Gate (or St. Stephen's Gate). "Ecce homo" translates as "Behold the man!" the words Pilate spoke in handing over Christ, crowned with thorns, to his accusers (John 19:5 NIV).

This is the first Station of the Cross, where

Christ stood before Pontius Pilate, who condemned Christ to death, then washed his hands of innocent blood. "When Pilate saw that he was getting nowhere, but rather that instead an uproar was starting, he took water and washed his hands in front of the crowd. 'I am innocent of this Man's blood,' he said. 'It is your responsibility!' " (Matthew 27:24 NIV).

From there the procession of worshipers, led by someone carrying a huge wooden cross as well as many other people (each carrying their own cross), continues up through the center of the Old City toward the Church of the Holy Sepulcher at Golgotha, stopping at certain points to commemorate notable moments of Jesus' journey.

These are the customary fourteen Stations of the Cross, generally based on verses in the four gospels, notably in Matthew 27, Mark 15, Luke, 23, John 18–19. A few are included by tradition only and are not mentioned in Scripture (as noted below).

Stations of the Cross

Jesus is condemned to die.

Jesus is given his cross to bear.

Jesus falls for the first time. (tradition only)

Jesus meets his mother. (tradition only)

Simon of Cyrene carries the cross for Jesus.

Veronica wipes Jesus' face with her veil. (tradition only)

Jesus falls for the second time. (tradition only)

Jesus meets the women of Jerusalem.

Jesus falls for the third time. (tradition only)

Jesus is stripped of his garments by soldiers.

Jesus is nailed to the cross.

Jesus dies.

Jesus is taken from the cross.

Jesus is laid in his tomb.

In Italy, the seat of Roman Catholicism, the Pope leads the Good Friday procession from *Il Colosseo* (the coliseum) to the Vatican. Throngs of Christians from many different countries attend.

Smaller processions take place in countless towns and villages across Italy to commemorate the crucifixion. Each one is usually led by men carrying an image of Christ (either on the cross, or lying down as if deceased), and includes prayers being recited aloud, sad songs, and people carrying lit candles. Some men also don robes and hoods as a sign of their penitence.

In smaller Italian villages, a faux tomb is erected in church and put under guard from Good Friday until Easter morning (as a kind of reenactment of the Roman guards at Christ's tomb). Parishioners visit throughout Holy Saturday and for Sunday services. Afterward everyone returns home to enjoy feasts in celebration of the Resurrection.

Fireworks for Jesus

Saturday to Saturday in Greece

Don't be alarmed, he said "You are looking for Jesus the Nazarene, who was crucified. He has risen! He is not here. See the place where they laid him."

Mark 16:6 RSV

Instead of starting on Palm Sunday, Holy Week in Greece and on the nearby island of Crete begins on the day before Palm Sunday, which is known as the Saturday of Lazarus. "The dead man came out, his hands and feet wrapped with strips of linen, and a cloth around his face. Jesus said to them, 'Take off the grave clothes and let him go'" (John 11:44 NIV).

This opening weekend of Easter Week

precedes church services held every night for the faithful, with a particular emphasis on Holy Tuesday, Good Friday, and Holy Saturday. Thursday is when everyone dyes Easter eggs red to represent the blood that Christ shed for humanity.

On Friday, worshipers place an image of Christ on a bier (a representation of a tomb) and process with it through the streets in the evening. They traditionally decorate it with garlands of flowers, and those in the procession hold brown candles symbolizing the cross of Christ.

Saturday is marked by preparation for Sunday dinner, which usually consists of lamb and a special Easter soup (mayiritsa) made from the lamb's offal (organ meats including liver, heart, lungs, tongue).

At night, the faithful attend a late-night church service, where just before midnight the church extinguishes all the lights and observes a brief silence. When the lights come back on, the priest in gold robes (rather than in the black robes associated with Good Friday) proceeds outside followed by churchgoers carrying white candles burning to represent the light of Christ.

At midnight they all shout *Christos Anesti!* ("Christ has risen!") Everyone hugs each other and rejoices. Christians set off fireworks, ships in the harbor blare their horns, floodlights illuminate the streets, and songs of praise ring out.

On Sunday, families party and feast on classic Greek dishes: lamb and lamb soup, chicken, shrimp with feta cheese, lemon butter cookies/biscuits, feta appetizers, and special breads.

A New Life; A New Look

Preparing for the Resurrection

When we walk, hand in hand, in the Easter Parade.

William Jay Smith
American poet

The Christian custom of wearing one's best clothes on Easter dates to the fourth century, when candidates for baptism at Easter/Pascha put on white robes for their immersion in the water. After baptisms, they would remain in the robes all week for the public to see as an outward sign of their inner transformation through Christ. "They will walk with me, dressed in white, for they are worthy" (Revelation 3:4 NIV).

It was called "White Week" (or "Bright Week" in the Eastern Orthodox Church) and served as a tangible reminder of the many commitments to Christ made in a particular city. Those who had already experienced baptism would also dress in a special way—not in white robes, but in new clothes as a way of sharing in the new life of the converts. Consequently, it is still customary for Christians to wear their best clothes on Easter, if not new clothes.

As for donning an Easter bonnet, this is no longer quite as popular as it was in the nineteenth and early twentieth centuries. The Easter parade, however, along with the sporting of new clothes, continues in many cities throughout the world, including New York.

At first glance, the Easter parade might seem little more than a showy, worldly practice that smacks of carnal pride and materialism. Indeed, the origins of the parade are in the pagan processions during the spring festival. Pagans believed wearing new apparel would bring good luck in the new season. And secular parades today, generally speaking, are also far more about the latest fashions than anything else.

The practice, however, can take on a Christianized spin for any churches that want to hold their own Easter parade (perhaps for children), if they recall the orthodox origins of the practice.

On the Horizon

Seeing God in the Sunrise

The city does not need the sun or the moon to shine on it, for the glory of God gives it light, and the Lamb is its lamp. The nations will walk by its light, and the kings of the earth will bring their splendor into it.

Revelation 21:23–24 NIV

One of the most long-standing symbols of Christ at Easter is that of the sun, which represents light, warmth, healing, truth, and life. The sun is associated with God in the Old Testament, which plainly declares, "[T]he Lord God is a sun and shield" (Psalms 84:11 NIV). The Messiah, too, is directly linked to the sun, where he is referred to as the "sun of righteousness" that will "rise with healing in its wings" (Malachi 4:2 NIV). "This draws on the imagery of the sun as a source of life," says the *Dictionary of Biblical Imagery.*

Easter sunrise ceremonies are based mainly on these two biblical verses, but they also came about to recall how the women discovered near sunrise that Jesus had been resurrected. "Very early on the first day of the week, just after sunrise, they were on their way to the tomb" (Mark 16:2 NIV).

Moreover, the picture of a literal sun rising at the beginning of Easter Sunday brings thoughts of a new beginning marked by brightness (resurrected life) coming out of darkness (death/grave).

The intensity of a new sun rising also brings to mind the promise given to Christians about the New Jerusalem, which will have no need of a sun because it will be lit by the brightness of the glory of God and the light of Christ (see Revelation 21:23–24 NIV on page 243).

The origin of sunrise ceremonies is in the original Easter Vigil on the Saturday night before Resurrection Sunday. In the early church, it lasted well into the early morning hours, and eventually grew so close to dawn that it finally was shortened and simply rescheduled to begin just prior to sunrise.

"[T]he service intends to celebrate the newness, the fresh possibilities, and new beginnings out of old endings that Jesus' resurrection embodies," writes Dennis Bratcher in "The Easter Season Resurrection of the Lord" from *The Voice* (www.crivoice.org/cyeaster.html, an ecumenical information source for Christians).

A pagan celebration closely resembled the modern Christian ceremony, but connecting them directly is beyond any evidence that exists. All we know is that the pagan sunrise ceremony was a way of welcoming the renewal of life at the spring equinox.

Today, however, Christians have supplanted this message with the good news of the gospel. It is one of the many ways early church leaders sought to turn the attention of pagans away from their beliefs and toward Christ.

Easter sunrise services, therefore, are no more "pagan" today than are modern wedding traditions that were formerly pagan (rings, cakes, gifts, veils) or the names for the days of the week (for example, Sunday, Monday, and Thursday, no longer mean, Sun's Day, Moon's Day, or Thor's Day in honor of the Norse God of Thunder).

Throughout the world, the sound of church bells also heralds the resurrection on Easter morning. In France and Italy, according to a legend told to children, the bells in all the churches go silent on Good Friday not only to signify mourning over the death of Christ, but also because they miraculously "fly away" to the Vatican in Rome.

They supposedly carry with them the sorrow and anguish felt by Christians over the crucifixion. Then, on Easter morning, the bells fly back to their places and ring aloud to announce the glorious Resurrection.

Oh, Happy Day!

And Now What, Lord?

By this gospel you are saved, if you hold firmly to the word I preached to you. Otherwise, you have believed in vain . . . that Christ died for our sins according to the Scriptures, that he was buried, that he was raised on the third day according to the Scriptures, and that he appeared to Peter, and then to the Twelve.

1 Corinthians 15:2–5 NIV

Belief in an afterlife permeates every culture. It is not surprising, therefore, that Christianity's wondrously Good News about the afterlife—the message of the "gospel"—appeals to so many individuals around the world, despite the many cultural and social differences that separate them.

"It is the power of God for the salvation of everyone who believes" (Romans 1:16 NIV).

Christianity offers a glorious hope—an eternity of peace and joy in the presence of our Creator in heaven. Christians rejoice over this future hope each year at Easter. Herein lies the powerful witness of Easter to the world.

The holiday enables faithful followers of Jesus to express to the world how, through Christ, it no longer has any reason to fear death. Easter is testament to the greatest gift ever given to humanity—forgiveness for our sins and eternal life. Or, as Paul the apostle phrased it, "Christ in you, the hope of glory" (Colossians 1:27 NIV).

For those who follow the Lord, a place where there will be "no more death or mourning" (Revelation 21:4 NIV) awaits them—a heaven with no more disease, broken relationships, unfulfilled dreams, or aging. Tears will be a thing of the past, and earthly tragedies such as famine will be forgotten, along with the pangs of hunger and thirst. "Never again will they hunger; never again will they thirst. The sun will not beat upon them, nor any scorching heat" (Revelation 7:16 NIV).

This spiritual domain, that Christians envision as their future home, is far more beautiful that the most exquisite place on earth. Consider the various benefits/blessings of heaven listed by author J. Oswald Sanders in *Heaven: Better By Far:*

- "We will enjoy eternal life in the immediate presence of the triune God."
- "All that diminishes the quality of life on earth will be banished. . . ."
- "The heights of joy we have experienced on earth will be eclipsed. . . ."
- "We will be 'saved to sin no more.' Failure and its consequences will be no more."

- "No more will we be subject to temptations from the world, the flesh, and the devil."
- "Knowledge will no longer be limited."
- "Limitations of the body will hamper us no more."
- "Everything that would enrich our lives will be available."
- "Reunion with loved ones and the formation of new relationships [will take place]. . . ."
- "Heaven's music will far surpass earth's finest achievements in that realm."
- "There will be satisfaction for every holy and wholesome longing and aspiration."

These aspects of the Christian afterlife are wrapped up not only in Easter, but also in its symbols, traditions, and customs. The most powerful symbol, of course, is the empty tomb, the ultimate sign of both the resurrection and the whole of Christianity itself. That is because the resurrection, the reason for Easter, *is* Christianity.

Without the resurrection, there is simply no faith to embrace "And if Christ has not been raised our preaching is useless and so is your faith" (1 Corinthians 15:14 NIV).

This has been the consensus of all great Bible teachers and scholars. R. A. Torrey, for instance, noted: "The Crucifixion loses its meaning without the Resurrection. Without the Resurrection, the death of Christ was only the heroic death of a noble martyr; with the Resurrection, it is the atoning death of the Son of God. It shows that death to be of sufficient value to cover our sins, for it was the sacrifice of the Son of God."

The heart of Easter is celebrating the fact that Jesus truly did rise from the grave, and by doing so, conquered death and opened up the way for humanity to join him for all eternity in the presence of God the Father. As Christ himself declared, "I am the way and the truth and the life" (John 14:6 NIV).

He also told us never to let our hearts be troubled, and to trust him, promising: "In my Father's house are many rooms. . . . I am going there to prepare a place for you. And if I go and prepare a place for you, I will come back and take you to be with me that you also may be where I am" (John 14:1–3 NIV).

This is more than enough reason to celebrate at Easter. So, whoever you are, wherever you are, with my own heart full of the Easter spirit, I close with my deepest prayers that you will be blessed on the next Resurrection Day, and say with heartfelt rejoicing: *Glad Påsk, Frohe Ostern, Buona Pasqua, Wesolych Swiat, Joyeuses Pâques, Gelukkig Paasfest, Boa Pascoa, Hos Paskalya, Linksmu Velyku, God Påske, Felices Pascuas, Sretan Uskrs* . . . HAPPY EASTER!

References

Celebrating a Miracle

xx: J. Dwight Pentecost, *Things Which Become Sound Doctrine* (Grand Rapids: Zondervan, 1970), 159.

Marked for Redemption

8: "Ashes," in *Dictionary of Biblical Imagery* (Downers Grove, IL: InterVarsity Press, 1998), 50.

A Time of Sacrifice

13: Howard Sainsbury, "Lent," in *The New International Dictionary of the Christian Church* (Grand Rapids: Zondervan, 1978), 590.

14: Oswald Chambers, *My Utmost for His Highest* (Toronto: McClelland and Stewart Ltd., 1935).

14: T. J. German, "Lent," in *Evangelical Dictionary of Theology* (Grand Rapids, Baker Book House, 1996), 629.

Morning by Morning

46: Leon McKenzie, "Pagan Resurrection Myths and the Resurrection of Jesus," www.paganlibrary.com.

47: J.R.R. Tolkien, Letter to Milton Waldman, c. 1951, in Humphrey Carpenter, ed., *The Letters of J.R.R. Tolkien* (Boston: Houghton Mifflin, 1981), 147.

47–48: C. S. Lewis, quoted in Mark Eddy Smith, *Tolkien's Ordinary Virtues* (Downers Grove, IL: InterVarsity Press, 2002), 13.

48: J.R.R. Tolkien, *Tree and Leaf* (London: Allen and Unwin, 1964), 62–63.

48: C. N. Manlove, *Modern Fantasy* (London: Cambridge University Press, 1975), 163.

For This Purpose He Came

51: George Eldon Ladd, *A Theology of the New Testament* (Grand Rapids, MI: Eerdmans, 1993), 469.

52: Paul Enns, *The Moody Handbook of Theology* (Chicago: Moody Publishers, 1989).

53–54: R. C. Sproul, "Table Talk, An Ongoing Finished Work," *Tabletalk*, August 1992, 39.

You Were a Slave

55–56: Lawrence O. Richards, *Expository Dictionary of Bible Words* (Grand Rapids: Zondervan, 1991), 516.

57: Paul Enns, *The Moody Handbook of Theology* (Chicago: Moody Publishers, 1989), 323.

58: *Vine's Complete Expository Dictionary of Old and New Testament Words* (Nashville: Thomas Nelson, 1985), 515.

58: Fritz Rienecker, *A Linguistic Key to the Greek New Testament* (Grand Rapids: Zondervan, 1980), 655.

Skeptics among Us

71: Walter Martin, *Essential Christianity* (Ventura, CA: Regal, 1980), 63.

71: Ronald Gregor Smith, *Secular Christianity* (London: Collins, 1966), 103.

74: Louis Berkhof, *Systematic Theology* (Grand Rapids: Eerdmans, 1993), 346.

Did He Fake It?

80: Peter Kreeft and Ronald K. Tacelli, *Handbook of Christian Apologetics* (Downers Grove, IL: InterVarsity Press, 1994), 183–184.

83: David Strauss, *New Life of Jesus* (London: Williams and Norgate, 1879), vol. 1, 422; Ian Wilson, *Jesus: The Evidence* (New York: Harper & Row, 1984), 51.

83: *Journal of the American Medical Society*, 255, no. 11, March 21, 1986, quoted in Norman Geisler's *Battle for the Resurrection* (Nashville: Thomas Nelson, 1989), 76–77.

A Conspiracy Theory

85: Louis Berkhof, *Systematic Theology* (Grand Rapids: Eerdman, 1993), 348.

88: Peter Kreeft and Ronald K. Tacelli, *Handbook of Christian Apologetics* (Downers Grove, IL: InterVarsity Press, 1994), 185.

The Jesus Impersonator?

89–90: Hugh J. Schonfield, *The Passover Plot* (New York: Bernard Geis, 1965).

More Than a Spirit

96: Winfried Corduan, *Reasonable Faith* (Nashville: Broadman & Holman, 1993).

A Skeptic Believes

97: Wayne Grudem, *Systematic Theology* (Grand Rapids: Zondervan, 1994), 608.

98: E. M. Blaiklock, quoted in Josh McDowell, "Evidence for the Resurrection," *Southern California Christian Times*, April 1992, 9.

98: Thomas Arnold, quoted in McDowell, 9.

The Evidence Is In

100–101: Kirsopp Lake, quoted in Ted M. Dorman, *A Faith For All Seasons* (Nashville: Broadman & Holman, 1995), 226.

Just the Facts

109: Gleason Archer, *Encyclopedia of Bible Difficulties* (Grand Rapids: Zondervan, 1982), 347–348.

110: Alister McGrath, *Explaining Your Faith* (Grand Rapids: Baker Book House, 1995), 72.

Double Meanings

121: *Evangelical Dictionary of Theology* (Grand Rapids: Baker Books, 1984), 339.

123–124: Faith Wallis transl., *Bede: The Reckoning of Time* (Liverpool University Press, 1999), 54.

Heavenly Signs

130: Joseph Seiss, *The Gospel in the Stars* (Grand Rapids: Kregel Publications, 1884, 1999 reprint), 15.

131: E. W. Bullinger, *The Witness of the Stars* (Grand Rapids: Kregel Classics, 2 Edition, 1893, 2003 reprint).

All Creatures Great and Small

135: Friedrich Rest, *Our Christian Symbols* (Cleveland: The Pilgrim Press, 1982), 8.

The Flora of Easter

143: Jim Bishop, "Symbol of Suffering and Death Offer New Life" *EMU News*, March 22, 2005, www.emu.edu.

Believing in the Easter Bunny

161: Ruth M. Reichmann, "The Changing Role of Easter Eggs," available online.

161: Susan E. Richardson, *Holidays & Holy Days* (Ventura, CA: Regal Books, 2001).

162: Nick Brown, "Pascha: Festivities and Symbols," www.orthodoxresearchinstitute.com.

The Incredible, Edible Symbol

166–167: Tamra Andrews, *Nectar and Ambrosia: An Encyclopedia of Food in World Mythology* (ABC-CLIO, 2000).

168: Nick Brown, "Pascha: Festivities and Symbols," www.orthodoxresearchinstitute.com.

The Colors of Faith

172: Leland Rykan, "Colors," in *Dictionary of Biblical Imagery* (Downers Grove, IL: InterVarsity Press, 1998), 158.

What's So Good About Friday?

204: Chris Armstrong, "The Goodness of Good Friday," *Christian History Newsletter*, April 18, 2003, www.christianitytoday.com.

A New Fire

208: Herbert Thurston, "Paschal Candle," in *The Catholic Encyclopedia* (Appleton Co., 1911), online edition.

On the Horizon

244: Leland Rykan, "Sun," in *Dictionary of Biblical Imagery* (Downers Grove, IL: InterVarsity Press, 1998), 827.

245: Dennis Bratcher, "Easter Season Resurrection of the Lord," *The Voice*, an ecumenical information source for Christians, www.crivoice.org/cyeaster.html.

Oh, Happy Day!

251–252: J. Oswald Sanders, *Heaven: Better By Far* (Billy Graham Evangelistic Association, 1994), 22–23.

Permissions